Song and Its Fountains

† † †

By the Same Author

SONG AND ITS FOUNTAINS

BY

A.E.

"Explore the River of the Soul, whence or in what order you have come; so that although you have become a servant to the body, you may again rise to the Order from which you descended, joining works to sacred reason."

The Chaldean Oracles

PUBLISHED FOR
THE PAUL BRUNTON PHILOSOPHIC FOUNDATION
BY

LARSON PUBLICATIONS

First published in 1932 by
MacMillan and Co., Limited

This edition
Copyright © 1991
by the Paul Brunton Philosophic Foundation

International Standard Book Number: 0-943914-52-3
Library of Congress Catalog Card Number: 91-60195

Manufactured in the United States of America

Published for the
Paul Brunton Philosophic Foundation
by Larson Publications
4936 Route 414
Burdett, NY 14818 USA

96   95   94   93   92   91
10   9   8   7   6   5   4   3   2   1

INTRODUCTION

SONG and Its Fountains is an inspired "retrospective meditation" on the process of inspiration. It is immensely valuable to anyone seeking to understand or stimulate the creative and visionary powers of the psyche.

Though widely recognized as a pivotal figure in the Celtic literary renaissance and the emergence of modern Ireland, AE held no stock in art and literature—or anything else, for that matter—as ends in themselves. For him, they became noble and useful only insofar as they expressed or inspired some form of spiritual realization. "Art for art's sake," he wrote in a letter, "is considering the door as a decoration and not for its uses in the house of life." Monk Gibbon observed (in his foreword to *Letters from AE*), that "the key to AE's life is the fact that he had elected to be a student of esoteric wisdom, and that his interest in literature, in poetry, in painting and in practical affairs were all to a large extent rooted in this original impulse."

AE's dictum was "Seek on earth what you have found in heaven." Much of his central philosophy is expressed in a section of a letter he wrote to the *Irish Times* which says: "Ideals descend on us from a timeless world, but they must be related to time; for this world has its own good, and, if we do not render it its lawful rights, neither will it receive our message, and Heaven and Earth are divorced and both are wronged."

"AE" is a pseudonym for George William Russell, who was born in Lurgan, County Armagh, Ulster, on April 10, 1867, and formally educated at the Rathmines School in Dublin. He died in London on July 17, 1935, three years after the original publication of *Song and Its Fountains.*

Throughout his life, AE exuded an idiosyncratic charm, an astonishing blend of intuitive vision and robust earthy practicality that earned the admiration and devoted friendship of many of his contemporaries. At the turn of the century, he formed lifelong friendships, for example, with W.B. Yeats, George Moore, Lord Dunsany, and James Stephens. Among the many writers who first flourished under his editorial guidance were Frank O'Connor, Sean O'Faolain, Liam O'Flaherty, F.R. Higgins, L.A.G. Strong, and Patrick Kavanagh.

AE was not only a poet, painter, essayist, journalist, and editor, he was also an astute economist with a comprehensive understanding of agricultural problems. During Franklin D. Roosevelt's first administration, Secretary of Agriculture Henry Wallace invited AE to lecture in the United States on rural reorganization. Both the London *Times* and the *Irish Times* frequently gave him *carte blanche* for editorial comment on key political issues of his day.

AE's uncommon practicality was rooted in establishing conscious communion with an inner order of genius that utters through the individual wiser things than the individual consciously knows. His extensive studies of the sacred literatures of Christianity, Brahminism, Buddhism, Taoism, Hermeticism, Platonism, and Neoplatonism (most notably Plotinus) were all means to develop and strengthen this communion. He was constantly invigorated by writers like Emerson and Whitman who "have more permanent value . . . for they had something of the element of infinity in their being without which writers lose their hold over the imagination and which makes them belong to one wave in time however subtle or prodigal in humor they may be."

His influence on the development of an integral East-West spirituality is immensely larger than has yet been credited appropriately. Late in his life, for example, he advised the young Paul Brunton: "Why go off to the East for light? If you believe in a World-Soul, then it should be possible to sit down even in a town like Dublin and look within until you contact that World-Soul and so gain all the spiritual light you seek. But perhaps your destiny compels you to go, for I foresee that you have an exceptional work to perform in threshing the corn of Eastern wisdom for the sake of Western students." In his own monumental *Notebooks,* Paul Brunton often speaks with reverential fondness of AE as a "true Olympian . . . my beloved friend . . . that versatile Irishman [who] was a gifted painter as well as poet, economist as well as prose essayist, clairvoyant, seer, and, when I met him, more of a sage."

For AE, nothing could be more practical than finding new ways to embrace and express the "element of infinity" in the human heart. *Song and Its Fountains* is his best testimony to the success he had in doing so, and to the methods that worked for him.

This 1991 re-issuing of the original 1932 edition has been lightly edited. Spelling and punctuation have been modernized in its prose sections, and exceptionally long paragraphs have been broken into shorter ones to make text pages more visually accessible. Original spelling, punctuation, and versing, however, have been retained in all the poetry.

TO
VIOLET
AND
DIARMUID

SONG AND ITS FOUNTAINS

IN what follows I have tried to track song back to its secret fountains. As I have thought it unnatural to see together in galleries pictures unrelated to each other, or taken from the altars for which they were painted, so I have thought it unnatural for lyric to follow lyric in a volume without hint of the bodily or spiritual circumstance out of which they were born. I have here placed some songs in their natural psychic atmosphere. Those who cannot follow my reasoning may perhaps be amused or interested by the fantasy a poet built about his life and poetry.

A.E.

1

A CHILD sits on the grass or strays in darkening woods, and its first going inward in dream may make inevitable a destiny. When inner and outer first mingle, it is the bridal night of soul and body. A germ is dropped from which inevitably evolves the character and architecture of the psyche. It is seed as truly as if it were dropped into earth or womb. Only what is born from it is a spirit thing, and it grows up and takes its abode in the body with its other inhabitants, earth-born or heaven-born. There may be many other minglings of heaven and earth in childhood which beget a brood which later become desires, thoughts, or imaginations, but the earliest are the masters and they lie subtly behind other impulses of soul.

This I found many years ago when I began to practice a meditation the ancient sages spoke of. In this meditation we start from where we are and go backwards through the day; and later, as we become quicker in the retracing of our way, through weeks, through years, what we now are passing into what we did or thought the moment before, and that into its antecedent; and so we recall a linked medley of action, passion, imagination, or thought.

It is most difficult at first to retrace our way, to re-
member what we thought or did even an hour before. But
if we persist the past surrenders to us, and we can race
back fleetly over days or months. The sages enjoined this
meditation with the intent that we might, where we had
been weak, conquer in imagination, kill the dragons which
overcame us before and undo what evil we might have
done. I found, when I had made this desire for retrospect
dominant in meditation, that an impulse had been
communicated to everything in my nature to go back to
origins. It became of myself as if one of those moving
pictures we see in the theaters, where in a few moments
a plant bursts into bud, leaf, and blossom, had been
reversed and I had seen the blossom dwindling into the
bud. My moods began to hurry me back to their first
fountains.

To see our lives over again is to have memories of two
lives and intuitions of many others, to discover powers we
had not imagined in ourselves who were the real doers of
our deeds, to have the sense that a being, the psyche, was
seeking incarnation in the body. As a tribe of gay or dusky
winged creatures we followed might lead us home to their
nest, so a crowd of delicately colored desires led me back
to the moment in childhood when, about four or five years
of age, beauty first dawned on me.

I had strayed into a park, and I remembered how I lay
flat on grass, overcome by some enchantment flickering
about a clump of daffodils. A little later I read a child's
story, and in this what fascinated me was that the hero
had a magic sword with a hilt of silver and a blade of blue
steel. The word "magic" stirred me, though I knew not
what it meant, as if there were some being within me which
could foresee the time when the whole universe—from
wheeling stars to the least motion of life—would appear to

be wrought by, or depend on, the magic of some mighty mind. It lay in memory, that word, without meaning, until a dozen years later its transcendental significance emerged as a glittering dragon-fly might come out of a dull chrysalis. But the harmony of blue and silver at once bewitched me. I murmured to myself, "blue and silver! blue and silver!" And then, the love of color awakened. A few days later I saw primroses and laid the cool and gentle glow of these along with the blue and silver in my heart, and then lilac was added to my memory of colors to be treasured. And so, by harmony or contrast, one color after another entered the imagination. They became mine or were denied, as they could or would not shine in company with those delicate originals of blue and silver. This love of color seemed instinctive in the outer nature, and it was only in that retrospective meditation I could see that the harmonies which delighted me had been chosen by a deeper being and were symbolic of its nature and not of that unthinking child's.

I think it was because in the first contact of soul and body I could remember beauty was born, that later in life I accepted ideas, philosophies, and causes for the beauty they suggested, and I have always shrunk from any activity in which I could not see that magic thing.

As my meditation revealed to me the birth here of the aesthetic sense, so it revealed to me when the sympathy for revolt was born. I was lying on my bed, a boy of fifteen or thereabouts. The faculty of dreaming while I was awake had then become active, though I hardly know whether what I have to tell was a dream of the waking self or revelation from some more ancient inner being. In my fantasy I was one of the Children of Light in some ancestral paradise, and it was rumored to us there were Children of Darkness, and the thought of them was fearful and abhorrent to us. But I in my imagination had wandered far outside the circle of light into a wilderness of space, and, far from that paradise, I became aware of a dark presence beside me, and I trembled because I knew it was one of the Children of Darkness. But this being whispered gently to me, "We of the Darkness are more ancient than you of the Light," and, at the saying of that, I forsook my allegiance to the Light, and my whole being yearned to lose itself in that Divine Darkness. This imagination of boyhood long forgotten I rediscovered years after, in that retrospective meditation, as the company of thoughts marched back with me along the road I had travelled. I knew in this lay the root of my many revolts against accepted faiths, and how later I could write a flaming rhetoric on behalf of those in my own country who were in revolt against its orthodoxies: exulting over the soul,

> resolutely putting aside all external tradition and rule, adhering to its own judgement, though priests falsely say the hosts of the Everlasting are arranged in battle against it, though they threaten the spirit with obscure torment for ever and ever: still to persist, still to defy, still to obey the orders of another captain, that unknown deity within whose trumpet-call sounds louder than all the cries of men.

I wrote so fiercely because the idea of revolt had incarnated in the hot body of youth and the gentleness of the whisper from the divine darkness was forgotten; and I did not then know that every passionate energy which goes forth evokes at once its contrary or balancing power, and that wisdom lies in the transmutation or reconcilement of opposites, and, if we were gentle enough, the God would give us a star to lead. The spirit of revolt sank later to more mystical depths, but it was from that original fountain of

dream that many poems came like that I wrote where the
man cries to the angel:

They are but the slaves of Light
Who have never known the gloom,
And between the dark and bright
Willed in freedom their own doom. . . .
Pure one, from your pride refrain,
Dark and lost amid the strife,
I am myriad years of pain
Nearer to the fount of life.
When defiance fierce is thrown
At the God to whom you bow,
Rest the lips of the Unknown
Tenderest upon my brow.

In that retrospect, too, I regained memory of the
greatest of all wonders in my boyhood, when I lay on the
hill of Kilmasheogue and Earth revealed itself to me as a
living being, and rock and clay were made transparent so
that I saw lovelier and lordlier beings than I had known
before, and was made partner in memory of mighty things,
happenings in ages long sunken behind time. Though the
walls about the psyche have thickened with age and there
are many heavinesses piled about it, I still know that the
golden age is all about us and that we can, if we will, dispel
that opacity and have vision once more of the ancient
Beauty.

There was another divine visitation in boyhood when
I was living in the country and was told of a woman who
was dying, how, a quarter of an hour or so before she went,
she wept that she was unable to rise and nurse a sick
neighbor; and there came on me a transfiguring anguish
because of this self-forgetfulness of hers, and though the
mood was too high for me to sustain, and I passed from it

to many egoisms, yet this was the starting-point of whatever selflessness was in my life. Yet because the love of beauty was the first-born of the union between soul and body I could never be like Plotinus and place the good above the beautiful.

One after another the desires and idealisms of later life were, in that retrospect, traced back to their fountains. There grew up the vivid sense of a being within me seeking a foothold in the body, trying through intuition and vision to create wisdom there, through poetry to impose its own music upon speech, through action trying to create an ideal society, and I was smitten with penitence because I had so often been opaque to these impulses and in league with satyr or faun in myself for so many of my days.

Yet this meditation, which discovers another being within us, unites us to it in some fashion; and in retrospect we seem to have lived two lives, a life of the outer and a life of the inner being. I do not know indeed, but I suspect of that inner being that it is not one but many; and I think we might find if our meditation were profound that the spokes of our egoity ran out to some celestial zodiac. And, as in dream the ego is dramatically sundered into This and That and Thou and I, so in the totality of our nature are all beings men have imagined—aeons, archangels, dominions and powers, the hosts of darkness and the hosts of light— and we may bring this multitudinous being to a unity and be inheritors of its myriad wisdom.

As I tracked the congregation of desires in myself back to its fountains in childhood I began to see too in those with whom I was intimate that each had some governing myth, that somewhere in their past, from the first bridal of soul and body, a germinal mood had been born which had grown to dominion over everything else in them. I can see today the central idea I surmised forty-five years ago in the young Yeats grown to full self-consciousness. I remember as a boy showing the poet some drawings I had made and wondering why he was interested most of all in a drawing of a man on a hilltop, a man amazed at his own shadow cast gigantically on a mountain mist, for this drawing had not seemed to me the best. But I soon found his imagination was dominated by his own myth of a duality in self, of being and shadow. I think somewhere in his boyhood at the first contact of inner and outer he became aware of a duality in his being. In his earlier poetry, one could pick out twenty lines showing how he was obsessed with this myth, how frequently and almost unconsciously the same idea recurs.

> Never with us where the wild fowl chases
> Its shadow along in the evening blaze.

or

> A parrot swaying on a tree
> Rages at its own image in the enamelled sea.

or

> Nought they heard for they were ever listening
> The dewdrops to the sound of their own dropping.

or

> The boy who chases lizards in the grass,
> The sage who deep in central nature delves,
> The preacher waiting the ill hour to pass,
> All these are souls who fly from their dread selves.

There are many such images in his early poetry. Then the mood ceased to haunt individual lines but became the subject of a long poem. I remember when we were walking along Leinster Road his telling me the first conception of

The Shadowy Waters. His hero, a world-weary wanderer, was trying to escape from himself. He captures a galley in the waters. There is a beautiful woman among the captives. He thinks through love he may have this escape and casts a magical spell on Dectora, but he finds the love so created only echoes back to him the imaginations of his own heart of which he is already weary, and in the original form of the poem he unrolled the spell and went alone seeking for the world of the immortals. I think when the poet came himself to love, the thought of that lonely journey to the Everliving grew alien to his mood; and the poem was altered, losing, as I think, the noble imaginative logic of its first conception, for in the new ending the love won by the magic art becomes an immortal love. Concealed or unconcealed, this preoccupation of the poet with that dualism of being and shadow is in much that he has written, until at last it becomes self-conscious in the *Vision,* a gigantic philosophy of self and anti-self.

I asked him could he remember at what moment in boyhood he was first conscious of this duality. But the poet is creative rather than introspective, and I do not think he had noticed how his final philosophy lay in germ in his earliest imaginations. There must have been many other contacts of inner and outer in his boyhood, for there are many colored threads woven in the rich tapestry of his poetry.

I think if we were truly wise in our analysis we could discover those dominant moods, and we might almost re-create for ourselves how in some reverie in childhood by river or road, in wood or on hill, faery first nodded at him, or how, and awakening what desire, the Mystical Rose opened first a burning blossom in his imagination.

I can surmise the character of the first illumination in Wordsworth, the most retrospective of poets, who knew also that in those illuminations a being was seeking incarnation in him, and in Shelley, Keats, and other poets when they were first met by their souls. I rarely see a child alone without wondering on what mysterious river consciousness is drifting. There is enchantment in those first adventures afloat on the canoe of dream, though the reverie may be like that doomful slumber Keats imagined.

> A poor Indian's sleep
> While his boat hastens to the monstrous steep
> Of Montmorenci.

The child does not know the distant thunder of the deep he goes to, which brings not a flutter to his heart that dreams. We cannot waken the dreamer or point him out his fate. That is ordained by the past, for the soul in its first kiss of the body renews an ancient love; and in this kiss, however gentle, are all the desires which brought it back to the world.

> Call not thy wanderer home as yet
> Though it be late.
> Now is his first assailing of
> The invisible gate.
> Be still through that light knocking. The hour
> Is thronged with fate.
>
> To that first tapping at the invisible door
> Fate answereth.
> What shining image or voice, what sigh
> Or honied breath,
> Comes forth, shall be the master of life
> Even to death.
>
> Satyrs may follow after. Seraphs
> On crystal wing
> May blaze. But the delicate first comer

It shall be king.
They shall obey, even the mightiest,
That gentle thing.

All the strong powers of Dante were bowed
To a child's mild eyes,
That wrought within him that travail
From depths up to skies,
Inferno, Purgatorio
And Paradise.

Amid the soul's grave councillors
A petulant boy
Laughs under the laurels and purples, the elf
Who snatched at his joy,
Ordering Caesar's legions to bring him
The world for his toy.

In ancient shadows and twilights
When childhood had strayed,
The world's great sorrows were born
And its heroes were made.
In the lost boyhood of Judas
Christ was betrayed.

Let thy young wanderer dream on,
Call him not home.
A door opens, a breath, a voice
From the ancient room,
Speaks to him now. Be it dark or bright,
He is knit with his doom.

2

WHILE I was yet a boy I began to run in and out of the house of dream, and as I went inward I grew older. An age of the spirit would fall upon me, and then I would come out of reverie and be the careless boy once more. Yet something of that ancientness of the psyche within clung to the boy, and began to part me from the thoughts of those about me. I at last realized with a kind of anguish that I was becoming a solitary, that a gulf had widened between myself and normal human life, between myself and home and love, the things in which most find a rich content. In the house of dream I entered there was neither home nor love, but beyond me in its labyrinths were intimations of primaeval being and profundities like the Pleroma. That myth of the Children of Light and the Children of Darkness was only one of many such myths telling in symbol of dawn-distant antecedents of human life, of revolts in heaven and the descent of the spirit to earth. They were strange inhabitants of the soul of the boy, for, when I first was visited by such imaginations, there was nothing in the culture with which I was familiar which might give birth to them.

Looking back on the past I have vivid sense of a being seeking incarnation here, beginning with those faint first intuitions of beauty, and those early dreamings which were its forerunners. It was no angelic thing, pure and new from a foundry of souls, which sought embodiment, but a being stained with the dust and conflict of a long travel through time, carrying with it unsated desires, base and august, and, as I divined of it, myriads of memories and a secret wisdom. It was not simple but infinitely complex, as a being must be which has been in many worlds and all it has experienced has become part of it. If there was an original purity of being it had become corrupted—yet not altogether, for there was in it, I believe, some incorruptible spiritual atom, carrying with it maybe some memory of its journeyings with deity. It had worshipped in many houses of prayer and kept the reverence it had paid, and had been in many a gay and many a ruined heart. Out of ancient happiness it could build intoxicating images of life, and out of ancient sorrows it could evoke a desolating wisdom that would crucify the infant joy ere it could run to its light.

It was such a being I surmised within me, trying to tune the body to be sensitive to its own impulses by a glamour cast upon desire, and also by vision, dream, and the illuminations of intuition and conscience. They impelled often in such contrary directions these impulses, that I divined a dual nature in the psyche. It was a being in part avidly desirous of life, while another part was cold to this, but was endlessly seeking for the Spirit.

I am going to set down as clearly as I can a record of some of these inbreathings, so that it may be seen out of what argument with myself I came to think as I do of the psyche as a being pre-existent to the body and seeking incarnation in it. I have already in *The Candle of Vision* tried to illuminate that nature normally invisible to us. But I was there intent on images which had form, because it is easier to reason over things which have shape and body than about bodiless things.

Intuition, feeling, thought are too swift in their coming and going, too elusive for a decisive argument over their nature. Though they may shake us by what they import, though what they in an instant hint at may be sacred to us, their coming and going are too swift for precise thought about themselves. In normal thought the fusion between inner and outer is so swift that it deceives the most attentive sense into the idea of unity, and we come to believe that there is no other creator of thought than the thinker who resides in the brain, who is with us from moment to moment, and we do not know what rays from how many quarters of the heavens are focused on the burning point of consciousness.

I had brooded much, hoping to weave a net which would hold these glittering visitors long enough for argument over where they were born and the manner of their coming. Then I remembered that a poem is the most intricately organized form of thought, and in the coming into being of poetry there is the greatest intensity of consciousness. Here we can recall more of the circumstance of creation than we can about more transient intuitions and ideas, though what they had to tell us may have been more profound than the thought which took shape in a lyric and remained with us. I could remember enough of the circumstance in which a lyric was born to weave an argument over it as I could about the images we see in vision or dream.

In dream there is a dramatic sundering of the psyche. One part of us is seer and another is creator. The seer of dream is unconscious of creation. He looks on the forms which appear as he might look on a crowd drawn together by impulses not of his creation. He does not think all this when he dreams, but, when he wakens and remembers, he knows that the creator of dream had a magical power transcending anything which he could do in his waking state. It can project crowds of figures, set them in motion, make them to move with perfect naturalness and wear the fitting expression for the deeds they do. Yet in the waking state of the dreamer, let him be given canvas, paints, and brushes, and he might boggle as a child would over the drawing of a figure. The creator in dream is swift inconceivably. What seems a long dream to the seer of dream often takes place in an instant, and may be caused by sound or touch which wakens him. Transformations, too, take place in dream which suggest a genius to which psychic substance is instantly malleable. If I tell a dream I had it may make this clearer.

In this dream I found myself in a room crowded with objects of art. Set apart on an easel was a picture. I looked at it and I wondered within myself how the artist painted so marvelous a sky. Then in my dream the painting, which was about two feet in length, was on the instant enlarged to about six feet, and every color the artist had used was left isolated from every other brushful of paint with a space of white canvas between each. I looked closely and saw that the dusky luminous sky I had wondered at had been made so to glow by touches of a pale rose violet laid alongside touches of a pale bluish green, each color keying up its delicate contrary. This dream I remembered, and I tried to make a replica of the picture the next day.

Is there not something beyond reason, something magical, in that swift analysis transfiguring the dream picture in response to a silent desire? You may say I, as an artist, must have known Monet and his school made scientific use of pure, broken, and contrasted color. But my dream was not thinking about a technical theory. The essential thing about it was that it was a vision. I was looking on a picture I could see clearly; and then came the astonishing enlargement of it, the analysis of color, every brushful of paint isolated, with the untouched white of the canvas showing between touch and touch.

The seer in dreams is apart from the creator. It is not

unreasonable to surmise an intellectual creator able to work magically upon psychic substance. Sometimes, indeed, at the apex of dream I have almost surprised the creator of it peering in upon me as if it desired by these miracles to allure me to discovery of itself. In the exploration of dream we acquire some knowledge of the workings of that mysterious psyche. And at times in the making of poetry I have been able to discover the true creator of the poem withdrawn far within from the waking consciousness. The poem seemed like an oracle delivered to the waking self from some dweller or genie in the innermost.

I propose to tell what I could discover about that psyche from the oracles I received and the manner of their coming. I think there should be as much interest in the truth about the making of a thing as in the thing that is made. If I choose to speak about my own poetry it is not because I think it is so fine a thing that what I say about it should be of interest to others, but because in the making of poetry I discovered, as I did in the exploration and analysis of dream, something about the nature of that psyche which began incarnating in me in early boyhood. Though I think in all speech, even the lightest, there is, in final analysis, mystery as profound as there is in the lordly speech of the prophets, I choose to speak about the making of poetry because, by reason of the intensity of consciousness involved in its making, I could remember more of the circumstance than that about ordinary speech, and was more aware of the duality in my being, of the interactions between inner and outer, and of the same mystery in its making as there is in the creation of dream. For those who cannot follow with confidence my reasoning, there may be some interest or amusement in studying the fantasies a poet built about his life and his poetry.

3

HOW is poetry born in us? There is, I think, some commerce between the outer and an inner being. Some character in aspiration determines the character of inspiration. In our meditation we are all consciously or unconsciously votaries of the Holy Breath. Our meditation is sacrifice and some one of its tongues of intellectual fire descends upon us. Saint Paul says there are diversities of powers but they all spring from the same Breath. To one may come the discerning of spirits, to another speaking with tongues, which I interpret to have, among others, these meanings: poetry, music, eloquence. In my imagination of his wisdom the purified psyche is a focus or burning point through which that which is in itself infinite or boundless manifests as pure light through a prism does, becoming sevenfold; and these intellectual fires are for ever playing upon us, and we apprehend them as wisdom, thought, power, love, music, or vision. By whatever way we ascend to that spirit it answers. I think poetry is one way in which it answers aspiration, and we receive, interpret, or misinterpret the oracle as our being here is pure or clouded.

To me it was only after long reverie that a song would come as a bird might fly to us out of the vast hollows of the air. I sometimes felt like that Merlin of legend who mused long by the margin of the great deep before a ninth wave bore the infant Arthur to his feet. There was always an element of the unexpected in the poetry itself, for it broke in upon and deflected the normal current of consciousness. I would be as surprised at the arising within me of words which in their combination seemed beautiful to me as I would have been if a water-lily had blossomed suddenly from the bottom of a tarn to make a shining on its dark surfaces. The words often would rush swiftly from hidden depths of consciousness and be fashioned by an art with which the working brain had but little to do.

Many poems were the residue or essence of waking dream. It is not true that we must fall asleep to dream. The dream consciousness may flood the waking, and that waking consciousness may have little more to do with the molding of the dream than the seer of dream in sleep has to do with the creation of the images by which he is surrounded. The waking dream may be likened to a living creature which invades us and obliterates all else in us until it has told its story. As a boy, I was often overpowered by waking dreams; and their intensity was such that in them I would forget myself and the earth I walked on, and be in another nature, or thousands of years behind time.

Some of these dreams were symbolic, and I surmise of others that they were memories of ancient life, or of experience which after death had gone into the heavenworld, and had there been thrice refined until little remained but essence that had become part of an immortal memory: and out of that enduring memory they were breathed into the mind of the boy to give age or wisdom to his thought, or to bring the being who lived today to some unity of purpose with the ancestral selves.

These waking dreams would fall upon me at any time, while I was at work, or in the streets, or in the country roads at night. Once I was walking down a passage in the great building where I was employed over forty years ago, a passage which led from one office to another; and in that dim lighted corridor my imagination of myself was suddenly changed, and I was a child and was looking upwards to a dawn of faintest yellow behind snowy peaks made blue and shadowy by that glow. The mound on which I stood was brown and bare as if it had been baked by the heat of fierce suns. The boy I had become was gazing in adoration at the high and holy light. He was celestially transparent, pure and virgin. He chanted a divine name, and a fire that was heaven-born leaped up from the heart, and for an instant the child was a delicate lyre whose strings quivered echoing the song of Brahma. Then all that faded and I was again in the offices at Pims; and I am afraid for the moment I was not doing their work, but was finding words which might hold that remote ancestral memory:

> Faint grew the yellow buds of light
> Far flickering beyond the snow,
> As, leaning o'er the shadowy white,
> Morn glimmered like a pale primrose.

Before that glamour had obliterated the corridor I was intent on the work I had to do, and this interruption of vision was like the sudden flowing into a cloudy river of crystal clear water from some tributary descending from high hills.

I must tell some other waking dreams before I can begin my speculation in regard to them. In such a waking vision I passed out of an ancient city built by the sea. It was steeped in the jewel glow and gloom of evening. There walked with me a woman whose face I could not see, for my head was downcast and I was rapt in my musing. It needed not that I should lift my eyes to see an image that was burning in my heart. I had gone from body to soul in my brooding, and the image was nigher to the inner eyes than it could ever be to the waking sight. We passed beyond the city gates, walking silently along the sands to a distant headland. The sea and sand swept by my downcast eyes in phantasmal flowings troubling not my thought. We came at last to the headland, climbed up a little way and sat down, and still no word was spoken. The love which was in my heart drew me inwards, and I was breaking through one ring of being after another seeking for that innermost center where spirit could pass into spirit. But when the last gate was passed I was not in that spirit I adored, but trembled on the verge of some infinite being; and then consciousness was blinded and melted into unconsciousness, and I came at last out of that trance feeling an outcast on the distant and desert verge of things, though there was a cheek beside mine and I felt a wetness and I did not know whether it was the dew of night or weeping. Then the dream closed. I had learned to be still when such visitations came, not to alter, not to remold. It was as truly dream and uncreated by the waking consciousness as any of the images which visited me in sleep. The dream, which was burdened with such intensities of emotion, when it departed left behind a slight lyric which could not hold or hardly hint at the love which had passed from earth to heaven and had forgotten the love which gave it wings to rise.

> As from our dream we died away
> Far off I felt the outer things,
> Your wind-blown tresses round me play,
> Your bosom's gentle murmurings.

And far away our faces met
As on the verge of the vast spheres,
And in the night our cheeks were wet,
I could not say with dew or tears.

O gate by which I entered in!
O face and hair! O lips and eyes!
Through you again the world I win,
How far away from paradise!

Why was this dream projected into the waking consciousness? It was not drawn out by affinity with any earthly desire, for I had not then come to love in life. I do not think I could say of any of my earlier poems that I had learned in experience or suffering here what was transmuted into song. Indeed I would reverse the order and say rather that we first imagine, and that later the imagination attracts its affinities, and we live in the body what had first arisen in soul. I had the sense that that far-travelled psyche was, in this and other waking dreams, breathing into the new body it inhabited some wisdom born out of its myriad embodiments. In this dream I was warned that love was a tale which already had been told, and I must not be allured by the romance of love, and that even from the noblest beauty the wonder would die swiftly. There came to me many oracles out of the psyche with this wisdom in their music.

O beauty, as thy heart o'erflows
In tender yielding unto me,
A vast desire awakes and grows
Unto forgetfulness of thee.

or

Beauty, the face, the touch, the eyes,
Prophets of thee, allure our sight

From that unfathomed deep where lies
Thine ancient loveliness and light.

As the sun in high air may be splintered into many stars upon moving waters, so the intensity of that dream was reflected in many a river of emotion. I look back with sadness upon a wisdom which too often was unregarded. But another wisdom was born from the conflict between cold spirit and flaming heart. I was not strong enough to go "alone to the Alone," but, if I could not be the ascetic mystic, neither could I be content with the contrary and competing passions. They gave something to each other, for the tenderness which is in our passionate earthly affections began to invade the heavens, and the heavens seemed to the imagination to glow with the infinite of all that here was brief and exquisite. What was gross divested itself of its sensual commonness to take on a beauty stolen from the spirit.

There is, I think, some necessity for the descents of the spiritual into the bodily to gather strength, while the demoniac in us is for ever trying to make captive spiritual beauty to sweeten its dark delights. I found, a melancholy wisdom, how many before myself had come to that perilous state where the evil in us has learned how to disguise itself in the apparel of light. It is vain to say the demon does not worship the beautiful. That worship is in almost all art and literature. It is in those strange heads drawn by Da Vinci where spirit and sense coexist in an almost sinister companionship in the same face, where there are lips that allure and eyes that are scornful. It is in the lovely faces painted by Rosetti where lips and burning eyes betray a thirst which could not be allayed in any spiritual paradise, or in lyrics of Heine, half-fairy, half-sensual. The tragedy of that mood was sung by Keats in *La Belle sans Merci*.

Halfway between spirit and matter there is a state where good and evil wear one face.

"There came and looked him in the face
An angel beautiful and bright,
And that he knew it was a fiend
That miserable knight."

They are the fortunate who know what dark passion may be hidden by the cheat of loveliness. Even when we think desire is left behind, on a sudden the desires we thought dead will rise from their grave in our meditation as if they were penitent, looking at us with angelic lips and eyes, and if we yield to their enchantment we may find they have become more terrible than when they were clothed in flesh. When desires die in the body they may reincarnate in the psyche, and may in our heavenward travelling fright us with terror as incubi or succubi.

4

IT may appear to many that I accept with a trust too easy
and complete whatever revelation may be in those waking
dreams. I have not passed the possibility that the psyche
may be a story-teller with its own art of glorifying its
memories. The ancient seers spoke of a state of soul
where, released from the heaviness of our life, and nearer
to its own divine root, memories of this life were transfigured,
or purified, until nothing remained but what had affinity
with its own immortality. And in telling these waking
dreams, which affected life and thought so much, I have
had in mind that possibility. But I was certain that they
were not creations of the waking consciousness. I was
sure of this, as I was sure that the seer in dream is not the
creator, and I felt I must explore into their origin.

I think there are many possible explanations. They
may be regarded as memories of past life, or as memories
transfigured in the psyche, or as symbolic dream, or as
moments in the lives of other beings attracted and related
to me by some mystical affinity in our natures. I think too
we may attract images to ourselves out of the book of life,
the memory of nature where they live "thinking the
thought and performing the deed." If I choose between
these interpretations I do so for the most part by indications

in myself which I find difficult to explain, though I will later try to make clear why I think some are ancestral memories—that is, connected in some way with the pre-existence of the psyche—and why some are transient fusions of my own consciousness with the consciousness of others. I noticed about these waking dreams that sometimes they would seem to be related to each other. That is, a second or third waking dream would seem to come out of the same remote life.

I had another lapse into that distant country where the young boy stepped out of a hut on the hillside to worship the dawn and chanted the ineffable name before it. In this the boy was on a hump of hill with other children. The hill sloped down into a vagueness below, where dimly a village could be seen veiled by its tresses of lazy smoke. And beyond this were the same mountains as the boy had seen at dawn. The children were in so lovely a mood of gaiety that the Golden Age might have been whispering its last in them ere it departed. To the boy the hollow of air was not empty but seemed filled with the bright ones, the devas, and he longed to be a sky-walker with them. His life was half with them and only half with his laughing companions. Then the mood in the boy changed from gaiety to one of fathomless sorrow, for something within him told him that the light of the world had gone out, the Iron Age had begun, and Earth was mourning in her deep heart. The last avatar of the spirit was dead, and nevermore or for long ages would there be any coming again of that hero. The sorrow of the long dead boy was recreated in the living; and by the living a song was made echoing the anguish of earth.

> Does the Earth grow grey with grief
> For her hero darling fled?

Though her vales let fall no leaf,
In our hearts the tears are shed.

Still the stars laugh on above;
Not to them her grief is said.
Mourning for her hero love,
In our hearts the tears are shed.

We, her children, mourn for him,
Mourn the elder hero dead.
In the twilight grey and dim,
In our hearts the tears are shed.

The dream was unfolding itself swiftly as in the vision of the boy at dawn. But it grew blurred ere it closed, for the waking mind would not be still, and began to take part that it might weave a story out of the unfolding dream and so broke its continuity. But it opened in perfect harmony with the earlier dream as if it were another episode of mystical childhood five thousand years ago.

I have noticed in other imaginations which came at different times a congruity with each other, as if characters and their setting were out of the same remote civilization. When the waking mind did not intervene, but was silently intent, the absorption at times would be as complete as if I had been in trance. Once I was moving in such a waking dream over a mountain road at night, absorbed by creatures of the imagination which held mystical converse with each other, and, when a man vaulted over a wall beside me, the thud of his feet on the path brought me back so violently from what a distance in time that my heart began an abnormal thumping, and I had to lean half-fainting against the wall to recover from that rude awakening.

I am trying to unveil some of the secret sources of poetry, and in what manner outer is molded by inner. And

I must tell yet another tale of glamour cast on the waking consciousness before I begin any speculation on it. In this I was parted from my normal self and had become another person, a kinsman in mood but unlike in circumstance. I was with a companion looking over a valley, a lovely land of woods and waters. And trees and lake, earth and air, seemed in the evening glow to be in a trance of still delight, that joy of nature when the mighty Master is busy with His art and His creations feel the molding touch of their creator. But I was shut out, exiled from intimacy with that myriad beauty, the life which breathed everywhere subtle and penetrating, which brought all but the gazer into unity with itself. I was shut out, for I had been traitor to earth and had forgotten it, having been long at other labors. Then a yearning had arisen in me to revisit the places of childhood, but the doors were closed to me. Earth denied me her blessing. I was no longer one of her children. Yet she had once, as I now knew, played in my heart, run in my limbs, and laughed through my lips. The things I had labored at in the city, which there seemed so mighty, here dwindled to the insignificance of dust beside the miracle of pure life I had lost, having fallen outside the circle of spirit. I realized this loss in an exquisite anguish in my heart, and then my companion broke silence, she who had played with me here in childhood and had returned with me, and I knew that her reverie was filled with as deep a regret as my own, for she said sadly, "How innocent our childhood was!" Then the glamour of that tragic summer night was over and I was myself once more.

You may say that that man I dreamed of was not in essence different from the dreamer. Yet while the glamour was on me I was that man, and knew from what labors and from what a life he had come to revisit this place, and they were not my labors nor my life. It was only for an instant in that poignancy of regret, knowing then what he had lost, that the circles of our being intersected. I had no feeling that this waking dream recreated for me anything I had already endured in an anterior life. The residue of that dream was a poem I called *A Summer Night*.

Her mist of primroses within her breast
Twilight hath folded up, and o'er the west,
Seeking remoter valleys, long hath gone,
Not yet hath come her sister of the dawn.
Silence and coolness now the earth enfold,
Jewels of glittering green, long mists of gold,
Hazes of nebulous silver veil the height,
And shake in tremors through the shadowy night.
Heard through the stillness, as in whispered words,
The wandering God-guided wings of birds
Ruffle the dark. The little lives that lie
Deep hid in grass join in a long-drawn sigh
More softly still: and unheard through the blue
The falling of innumerable dew
Lifts with grey fingers all the leaves that lay
Burned in the heat of the consuming day.
The lawns and lakes lie in this night above,
Admitted to the majesty above.
Earth with the starry company hath part:
The waters hold all heaven within their heart
And glimmer o'er with wave-lips everywhere
Lifted to meet the angel lips of air.
The many homes of men shine near and far,
Peace-laden as the tender evening star.
The late home-coming folk anticipate
Their rest beyond the passing of the gate,
And tread with sleep-filled hearts on drowsy feet.
Oh, far away and wonderful and sweet

All this, all this. But far too many things
Obscuring, as a cloud of seraph wings
Blinding the seeker to the Lord behind,
I fall away in weariness of mind,
And think how far apart are I and you,
Beloved, from those spirit children who
Felt but one single Being long ago,
Whispering in gentleness and leaning low
Out of Its majesty as child to child.
I think upon it all with heart grown wild,
Hearing no voice, howe'er my spirit broods,
No whisper from those dense infinitudes,
This world of myriad things whose distance awes.
Ah me: how innocent our childhood was!

I had often at other times the sense that for an instant, an unforgettable moment, the circle of my being intersected with others, and that I had been admitted into the secrecy of other hearts. These people were all strange to me, men, women, or children, except at the point of intersection. It was not, I think, merely a transfer of images such as may take place in thought-transference.

I have told in *The Candle of Vision* how my mind was once flooded with images. There was an old man in a little shop, a red-haired watchful girl, a cobbled street outside; I might have supposed all this was only what we call imagination but that I had an impulse to question my office companion about his people, and I found I had seen his father and sister. I had really been adventuring in the mind of another. There was there no identity of emotion. It was only the transfer of images from an active to a vacant mind. But I brooded much over the limitless possibilities of that momentary clairvoyance, and when I came to have waking dreams like that of the statesman mourning over a lost intimacy with spiritual nature, I felt a conviction that consciousness had melted into unity with another being through some transient affinity of mood.

In thinking over such experiences, I have felt that not only are we fed out of an immortal memory but we have secret ties with the living. I can only interpret these experiences by accepting what Kant wrote:

> I am much disposed to assert the existence of immaterial natures in the world and to place my own soul in the class of these beings. It will hereafter, I know not where or when, yet be proved that the human soul stands even in this life in indissoluble connection with all immaterial natures in the spirit world, that it reciprocally acts upon these and receives impressions from them.

The truth of that will never, I think, be proved by any dialectic, but by experience when we may meet in the body those we have first known in the secrecy of spirit and speak to each other about the moment when soul was nearer to soul than our own bodies are to us. I had but one constant mood of preoccupation with the spirit; and but rarely in my meditation did I brood upon other things, and because of this the points of intersection or mingling with other souls were only at moments of spiritual gain or defeat.

I have often thought the great masters, the Shakespeares and Balzacs, endowed more generously with a rich humanity, may, without knowing it, have made their hearts a place where the secrets of many hearts could be told; and they wove into drama or fiction, thinking all the while that it was imagination or art of their own, characters they had never met in life, but which were real and which revealed more of themselves in that profundity of being than if they had met and spoken day by day where the truth of life hides itself under many disguises. When we sink within ourselves, when we seem most alone, in that solitude we may meet multitude. The psyche, when it has evolved a higher quality of that element which mirrors being, and by which it becomes self-conscious, may become not only aware of its own spirit but of that relation with other spirits which Kant divined. Here we may find one of the secret sources of drama, poetry, and wisdom. The psyche may, by the evolution of this sensitiveness, through love and sympathy, come to know that the whole of life can be reflected in the individual and our thoughts may become throngs of living souls.

5

THE sages who spoke of that retrospective meditation said also that by following it we could regain memory of past lives. The meditation does not bring us only to the fountains of beauty or desire or fear in this life. Wisdom, fear, desire have a remote ancestry, and if the meditation is intense enough it may recall what tragedy in the past gave birth to wisdom or fear in this life, what vision of the heavens revealed a new star by which the mariner might guide the barque of the soul.

When I was young, and these whisperings and breathings out of the past brought me to the belief that I was on a journey between two eternities, I was not content with spiritual memories but desired to know what else there was to be known, what kind of being walked in ancient cities, what its labors were, its loves, tragedies, and delights. But in this curiosity I was not sustained from within. When I sought for spiritual wisdom out of that ancestral memory I had the sense of being sustained, but not when I sought for the personal.

Once I was met by a terror frightening me from my meditation. In my brooding there had been born the sense that in some life before this there had been mighty happenings, aspirations, downfall, and a tragic defeat. I began a concentration on that intuition. But there was some wisdom within me greater than my own which stayed me, for I had hardly begun my meditation than I was enveloped by that terror I spoke of, the fear that there would be revelation of things I could not endure; the resurrection of tragedies and crucifixions of the heart; of things I had done which were awful and unspeakable, the punishment for which was yet to fall. I knew not what I had done, whether my will had dared to storm the heavens, and had been hurled back and had itself been broken, and in its madness had reversed its heaven-assailing desires and the divine powers had been turned to infernal uses, and even love had been crucified in its despair. I seemed to be warned that if I persisted in this meditation I would arouse dragons that lay in slumber. I would be beset by powers I was too feeble now to master, and they would make wreck of the life which was slowly gathering itself from that defeat of the spirit.

I was so overcome by this terror that I stayed the meditation, and a poem I had begun evoking that past was left uncompleted for thirty years. I could not continue it after two lines had come to my lips lest the very words might wind into their music the passion which once had made wreckage of the soul. It was only when I was old and desire had no power over me, that one day the poem completed itself. I do not think it was the poem I would have written if I had persisted in that tragic meditation. It had become wisdom rather than memory.

> Not by me these feet were led
> To the path beside the wave,
> Where the naiad lilies shed
> Moonfire o'er a lonely grave.

Let the dragons of the past
In their caverns sleeping lie.
I am dream-betrayed, and cast
Into that old agony.

And an anguish of desire
Burns as in the sunken years,
And the soul sheds drops of fire
All unquenchable by tears.

I, who sought on high for calm,
In the Ever-living find
All I was in what I am,
Fierce with gentle intertwined,

Hearts that I had crucified,
With my heart that tortured them—
Penitence, unfallen pride,
These my thorny diadem.

Thou wouldst ease in heaven thy pain,
O thou fiery, bleeding thing.
All thy wounds will wake again
At the heaving of a wing.

All thy dead with thee shall rise,
Dies irae. If the soul
To the Ever-living flies
There shall meet it at the goal

Love that time had overlaid,
Deaths that we again must die—
Let the dragons we have made
In their caverns sleeping lie!

This poem I call *Resurrection,* and it may explain why
I speak of certain poems as oracles out of the psyche. They
breathed out of some deep-remembered wisdom warning

or guidance, for when the words swam up into consciousness there was more in them than the waking self had thought or known. I divined from it that before the psyche can be absorbed in spirit—the son in the bosom of the Father—there must be resurrection of the past, a resurrection of memory of all the evil we have done, and that agony must be endured. After that may come the resurrection of what was lovely and beloved, of which I wrote elsewhere:

> I know when I come to my own immortal I will
>   find there
> In a myriad instant all that the wandering soul
>   found fair,
> Empires that never crumbled and thrones all
>   glorious yet,
> And hearts ere they were broken and eyes ere
>   they were wet.

It was from the early verses I wrote that I had the clearest conviction of something in the deeps of being wiser than myself, with an age in thought and emotion which was not at all in the waking consciousness. I have told how when I was a boy I began to run in and out of the house of dream, and as I went inward an age of the spirit fell upon me, and then I would come out and be the careless boy once more with all youth in his emotions and acts.

I must make plainer what I mean by this age of thought superimposed upon the outward nature. Sometimes, as I have said, the dream consciousness would flood the waking. At other times I would be drawn inward, and in that mid-world of the psyche there would arise not merely visions of things I held to be memories, but imaginations, tales, and myths would arise which were purely symbolic.

One of these early imaginations was a tale I wrote as
The Cave of Lilith. It was born swiftly within me. There were
three beings in the tale, an enchantress who symbolized
that Maya in which we look outside ourselves and gaze on
the mirror of being rather than on being itself. There was
a sad singer who symbolized the psyche caught in that
Maya, and there was a Wise One who symbolized the
Spirit. In my imagination Lilith the enchantress was ex-
ultant over the souls she kept in her cave, and she cried
out to the Wise One:

"My illusions are sweeter to them than truth. I offer
every soul its own shadow. I pay them their own price.
I have grown rich though the simple shepherds of old
gave me birth. Men have made me. The mortals have
made me immortal. I rose up like a vapor from their
first dreams, and every sigh since then and every
laugh remains with me. I am made up of hopes and
fears. The subtle princes lay out their plans of conquest
in my cave, and there the hero dreams, and the lovers
of all time write in flame their history. I am wise
holding all experience to tempt, to blind, to terrify.
None shall pass by me. The stars and the starry crown
are not yours alone to offer, and every promise you
make I make also. I offer the good and bad indifferently.
The lover, the poet, the mystic, and all who would
dream of the first fountain I delude with my mirage.
I was the Beatrice who led Dante upward. The gloom
was in me and the glory was mine also and he went
not out of my cave. The stars and shining of heaven
were illusions of the infinite I wove about him. A
nutshell would have contained the film. I smote on
the heart-chords the manifold music of being, God is
sweeter in the human than the human in God.
Therefore he rested in me. There is that fantastic

fellow who slipped by me. Could your wisdom not retain him? He returned to me full of anguish. I wound my arms around him like a fair melancholy, and now his sadness is as sweet to him as hope before his fall. Listen to his song." A voice came from the depths chanting a sad knowledge:

What of all the will to do?
It has vanished long ago,
For a dream-shaft pierced it through
From the unknown archer's bow.

What of all the soul to think?
Someone offered it a cup,
Filled with a diviner drink
And the flame has burned it up.

What of all the hope to climb?
Only in the self we grope
To the misty end of time.
Truth has put an end to hope.

What of all the heart to love?
Sadder than for will or soul,
No light lured it on above.
Love has found itself the whole.

This fragment of a tale may make clear the mystery of such imaginations, how going inward I would be met by myth and dream, and they would unfold themselves with a swift concentration—though at the time I wrote this poem and imagined this myth the outward self, as Yeats recalls in his Memories, was stumbling and chaotic in speech, and, as I know, as confused and stumbling in mind, until I went into those mysterious depths of consciousness where I found the psyche waiting to initiate me into its own wisdom.

There are many colored tributaries of the river of life here which flow into it from uncharted regions of being. How can we explain the mystery of imagination, the power we discover in ourselves which leaps upon us, becoming master of ideas, images, and words, taking control of these from the reasoning mind, giving to them symbolic meanings, until images, ideas and words, swept together, become an intellectual organism by some transcendental power superior to all reasoning? It is as mysterious as the growth of an organism in nature which draws from earth by some alchemy the essences it transmutes and makes subservient to itself. There was a greater age of thought in the imagination of *The Cave of Lilith* than there was in the outer mind, a wisdom which had ransacked the treasure-house of thought, but had grown weary because thought of itself leads nowhere, but blows the perfume from every flower, and cuts the flower from every tree, and hews down every tree in the valley, and in the end goes to and fro gnawing itself in a last hunger.

I will try later to give reasons why I infer an interior creator of poetry and myth, a being with pre-natal wisdom, which exists in all of us trying to become self-conscious in the body. There are two wisdoms in us, the wisdom we are born with and the wisdom we acquire. The outer mind grows but slowly to maturity, and even at its culmination it is never so wise as that other enriched by the garnered wisdom of countless lives. In the poetry of my boyhood there was, I think, some breathing of that inner wisdom. Its wisdom was not learned in any suffering here, and whatever anguish it may have been born out of lay far behind time.

When I was about twenty-eight I began rapidly to adjust myself to the life about me, to lose the old confused timidity, and to talk with easy assurance to others. But

while the outer mind became almost sage compared with
the rambling immaturity of the young man, my most
matured thought would seem young and immature
whenever the psyche breathed its own wisdom. I had the
gift of good health, the capacity to feel intense delight, and
I never had any outward satiety such as follows a too avid
thirst for pleasure. Yet, while the outer nature would be
rapt in its imagination of love, there would break in upon
its delight some oracle out of the psyche, a being to which
our delight in beauty here was but a play which had lost
meaning long ages ago.

> We are desert leagues apart,
> Time is misty ages now
> Since the warmth of heart to heart
> Chased the shadows from my brow.

> Oh, I am so old, meseems
> I am next of kin to Time,
> The historian of her dreams
> From the long-forgotten prime.

> You have come a path of flowers.
> What a way has mine to roam,
> Many a fallen empire's towers,
> Many a ruined heart my home.

> No, there is no comfort, none.
> All the dewy tender breath
> Idly falls when life is done
> On the starless brow of death.

> Though the dream of love may tire,
> In the ages long agone
> There were ruby hearts on fire—
> Ah, the daughters of the dawn!

Though I am so feeble now,
I remember when our pride
Could not to the Mighty bow.
We would sweep His stars aside.

Mix thy youth with thoughts like those—
It were but to wither thee,
But to graft the youthful rose
On the old and flowerless tree.

Age is no more near than youth
To the sceptre and the crown,
Vain the wisdom, vain the truth,
Do not lay thy rapture down.

I said I surmised a duality in the psyche, for the
oracles it delivered in song often seemed to lead to
opposing eternities. The wisdom before which love grew
chill would be opposed by oracles speaking of an immortal-
ity of love. At one moment the psyche would seem to be
redeemed from that passion; and then there would be an
illumination of vision, and desire and imagination would
be inflamed, and images would rush at me out of the deeps
of life as creatures which had been long beloved, and
which had been reborn to renew again their ecstasy. They
carried with them in fantasy the setting of their lives,
palaces and cities that had long crumbled into dust, and
I was as ready to yield to love as if it had been born for the
first time and had never known of its many cruelties and
anguishes. This which follows was written close on the
time when *The Grey Eros* was written.

The blue dusk ran between the streets. My love
was winged within my mind.
It left day and yesterday and thrice a thousand
years behind.

To-day was past and dead for me, for from to-day
    my feet had run

Through thrice a thousand years to walk the ways
    of ancient Babylon

On temple top and palace roof the burnished gold
    flung back the rays

Of a red sunset that was dead and lost beyond a
    million days.

The tower of heaven turns darker blue, a starry
    sparkle now begins.

The mystery and magnificence, the myriad beauty
    and the sins

Come back to me. I walk beneath the shadowy
    multitude of towers.

Within the gloom the fountain jets its pallid mist in
    lily flowers.

The waters lull me and the scent of many gardens,
    and I hear

Familiar voices, and the voice I love is whispering
    in my ear.

Oh, real as in dream all this; and then a hand on
    mine is laid,

The wave of phantom time withdraws, and that
    young Babylonian maid,

One drop of beauty left behind from all the flowing
    of that tide,

Is looking with the self-same eyes, and here in
    Ireland by my side.

Oh, light our life in Babylon, but Babylon has
    taken wings,

While we are in the calm and proud procession
    of eternal things.

In that fierce illumination which gave birth to the
poem, I was surrounded by a wavering of phantom pictures.

A dusky beauty all in rose and gold flowed to me. There were high buildings, strange cars or chariots, a great room with stone walls and an iron door, as if the whole of some gorgeous past wished to renew itself at that instant. Years after I read about some half-buried city in Bashan that the iron doors were still in the stone walls.

Here were voices out of the deep of being, an Eros that seemed to have run its race, and an Eros eager as if it ran to meet its first love. I have found this duality in everything in my life, and I can only surmise some wisdom, above the outworn heart and the eager heart, which understands that we cannot be wholly of this world or wholly of the heaven-world, and we cannot enter that Deity out of which came good and evil, light and darkness, spirit and matter, until our being is neither one or the other, but a fusion of opposites, a unity akin to that Fullness where spirit, desire, and substance are raised above themselves and exist in that mystic unity of all things which we call Deity.

6

I HAVE spoken of certain poems as oracles out of the psyche, by which I imply they were conceived and fashioned by some high part of our dramatically sundered being and were breathed into the waking consciousness. I realize that what I have already written might have other interpretations, though I have never been able to explain the flooding of the waking consciousness with a dream story otherwise than by assuming it was a projection from a genie in some deep of our being. But at other times I found the relation between inner and outer not so debatable. I woke up one morning and some lines of verse tumbled out of the dream state into the waking.

> A wind blew by from icy hills,
> Shook with cold breath the daffodils,
> And shivered as with silver mist
> The lake's pale leaden amethyst.
>
> It pinched the barely budded trees,
> And rent the twilight tapestries,
> Left for one hallowed instant bare
> A single star in lonely air.

After these followed a line which seemed to have no relation to the preceding lines:

The city with its burning piles.

I had an instinct that rather a long poem had been completed in dream, and that all I had to do was let the poem drift into consciousness. Walking about the hills, in a few days the poem was completed. After about two hundred lines had been written down

The city with its burning piles

fell into its proper place, and the plan of the poem *Michael* first became clear to myself. I noted that towards the close of the poem there were some verses suggesting that the real fountain of many acts lay in the kingdom of sleep.

For many a one a tryst has kept
With the immortal while he slept,
Woke unremembering, went his way,
Life seemed the same from day to day,
Till the predestined hour came,
A hidden will leapt up in flame,
And through its deed the risen soul
Strides on self-conquering to its goal.

Here at least was partial discovery in what region of our being was the foundry where poetry was fashioned. About eight or nine lines there could be no doubt. But at another time the revelation was complete. I was surprised by a sudden fiery rushing out of words from within me, and I took paper and pencil and wrote as rapidly as fingers could move the words which came to me; and I was aware from the first that all was complete, and the verses altogether seemed to float about the brain like a swarm of bees trying to enter a hive. It may be that they did not all find entry. I did not know what idea was in the poem until it was written down. It seemed to be a wild dialogue between the shadowy self and some immortal consciousness which was making vast and vague promises to the lower if it would but surrender itself to the guidance of that heavenly shepherd.

> "Who art thou, O glory,
> In flame from the deep,
> Where stars chant their story,
> Why trouble my sleep?
> I hardly had rested,
> My dreams wither now,
> Why comest thou crested
> And gemmed on thy brow?"

> "Up, shadow, and follow
> The way I will show.
> The blue-gleaming hollow
> To-night thou shalt know,
> And rise mid the vast to
> The fountain of days,
> From whence we had passed to
> The parting of ways."

> "I know thee, O glory,
> Thine eyes and thy brow,
> With white fire all hoary,
> Come back to me now.
> Together we wandered
> In ages agone,
> Our thoughts as we pondered
> Were stars at the dawn.
> My glory has dwindled;
> My azure and gold;
> Yet you keep enkindled

The sun-fire of old.
My footsteps are tied to
The heath and the stone,
My thoughts earth-allied-to.
Ah, leave me alone.
Go back, thou of gladness,
Nor wound me with pain,
Nor smite me with madness,
Nor come nigh again."

"Why tremble and weep now,
Whom stars once obeyed?
Come forth to the deep now
And be not afraid.
The Dark One is calling,
I know, for his dreams
Around us are falling
In musical streams.
A diamond is burning
In deeps of the Lone,
Thy spirit returning
May claim for its throne.
In flame-fringed islands
Its sorrows shall cease,
Absorbed in the silence
And quenched in the peace.
Come lay thy poor head on
My heart where it glows
With love ruby red on
Thy heart for its woes.
My power I surrender,
To thee it is due,
Come forth, for the splendour
Is waiting for you!"

I do not think it a very good poem whatever dream may be in it. Nor do I wish to distinguish my verses from the poetry of others as being communicated in any abnormal way, as I believe all poetry is born beneath the dream consciousness. I have only been more curious than others about the forge in which poetry is fashioned, and when, as in that wild dialogue between Glory and Shadow, I know that the waking consciousness had nothing whatever to do with the making of it, and not until it was written down did I know the purport of what was written, I could only assume an internal creator. In almost everything I wrote, even though the words did not rush so swiftly from inner to outer, I had this element of surprise in the uprising of poetry when the superficial consciousness is made brilliant by a light or power flooding it from within.

Where, then, are the ideas in poetry given an organic form? Where are the images we see in symbolic dream set in motion? Whence come vision and high imagination? I think they come from a center of consciousness behind the sphere of dream. Here I pass from experience to rely on intuition and the wisdom of others. It is to the seers who wrote the Upanishads I turn for illumination. They speak of four states of the soul—waking, dreaming, deep sleep, and spirit waking—the last a state in which the spirit is unsleeping in its ecstasy of infinite vision. I quote in what follows from an interpretation of my own of those four phases of soul the seers spoke of.

> The Vedic seers had a more grandiose tale
> Of what lay in the secrecy of sleep,
> The soul gone into itself, its gates
> Barred upon earth, earth's magic stilled within
> The sleepy mind, the candles of dream all blown.
> When sleep is dreamless the gold-gleaming genius

Awakens laughing, immortal, so they say,
Making music, chariot, dance and song,
Cities and palaces and lamps in heaven,
And meadows for the dancing feet, and lakes
Gaudy with light, and flaring forest glades
Where wind bewildered the mad sun-fire reels,
And rainbow-tinted the lovely dryads whirl
In carnival, a lustrous mirage for ever
Glowing and changing at the heart's desire,
As if the Arabian genii were its slaves.
And after that glorying in beauty and power
The genius becomes inexpressibly old,
Returning into the Ancient of Days. It must
As the diver under deep water must
Rise to the air for life, so every night
The soul must rise and go unto its Father,
For a myriad instant breathing eternity.
And then, returning by the way it came,
It wakes here to renew its cyclic labours.

In that mysterious journeying from time to eternity, where the soul moves on to ever higher planes of its own being, there must be many transformations of the psyche. Something I think goes with it from this world to that other. "The gods feed upon men." Something comes back with it from Heaven to Earth. "The gods nourish us."

There is, I believe, some commerce between this world and that other. As our aspiration is, so is our inspiration. The higher nature takes our fragmentary knowledge, thought, experience, and our aspiration, which is sacrifice, and it is transfigured, made whole and returned to us. What is earth-born is lifted up and perfected, shot through and through with the light of that higher world where the psyche nigh to its divine root imagines the perfection or truth in all things. Much must be lost of that transcendental lucidity and beauty of the heavenly consciousness when the psyche sinks through murky clouds of desire back to the body again. But something returns.

There are many I know who are not mystics who do yet before sleeping confide their questioning to a wisdom they divine is unsleeping while the body sleeps. The doctor is confirmed in his diagnosis. The scientist receives his flash of intuition about the laws of nature. The worshipper is endowed with inward peace, or the stirring of conscience tells him where he has erred and strayed. The poet feels the Magician of the Beautiful stirring in his imagination. It is, I think, in one of the higher transfigurations of the psyche beyond the mid-world of dream, in that phase where it is creator, that poetry is born. The seer of the Upanishads speaks of that state.

> There are no chariots there, nor streets for chariots. The soul makes himself chariots and streets for chariots. Nor are any delights there, nor joys nor rejoicings. The soul makes for himself joys and rejoicings. . . . For the soul of man is creator.

The words of the seer imply that there come up to that high world images of the earth-world, chariots, lotus ponds, joys and rejoicings; and, taking images and ideas, the god-lit psyche makes its magical play as a great poet transfiguring the things his eyes have seen and making of them a wonder-world of his own, of magic casements, perilous seas, and forlorn fairylands. Here, too, the soul being immortal, would be memories of its journeyings from the beginning of time, of religions and civilizations which are all built about some divine idea, some hope of liberty, power, or beauty breathed into men from the divinity which overshadows them. The soul returns by the way it came from those high spheres to the body to take up its labors in this world.

What are its labors? It has to make conquest of this world, become master of the nature which envelops us, until the eternal is conscious in us, and we have made this world into a likeness or harmony with the Kingdom of Light. As our being here becomes transparent to the Light we receive more and more of the true. Intuitions begin to leap up in us every instant, and we receive, according to our capacity, vision, imagination, knowledge of past and future, illuminations about the nature of things, wisdom and poetry. The fountain of all these lies deep within us where the psyche in ceaseless ecstasy responds to the Will that moves the universe and translates the wisdom of that being into the intellectual fires of the Paraclete, and its fiery tongues give the divine signature to our thoughts. The divine receives from the mortal and returns our sacrifice changed by some heavenly alchemy into sub-stances which have the divine signature upon them.

That high center within us where the images of earth are so glorified and returned to us I call the Mount of Transfiguration, and one of the earliest breathings out of the psyche which came to me spoke of this transfiguration.

> Those delicate wanderers,
> The wind, the star, the cloud,
> Ever before mine eyes
> As to an altar bowed,
> Light and dew-laden airs
> Offer in sacrifice.
>
> The offerings arise,
> Hazes of rainbow light,
> Pure crystal, blue and gold,

Through dreamland take their flight,
And mid the sacrifice
God moveth as of old.

In miracles of fire
He symbols forth His days,
In dreams of crystal light
Reveals what pure pathways
Lead to the soul's desire
The silence of the height.

7

EARTH does not give us more "sweet things out of our corruption" than the soul gives us for the dust of thought if it was gathered while we were travelling towards the Spirit. I know many will say if they knew all I had read or experienced before the poem was shaped they could find all the materials ready for fusion without calling on some high genie in consciousness to account for a lustre to me otherwise inexplicable. The effort to reassemble the ingredients of poetry pre-existing before the poem was made at immense length in *The Road to Xanadu,* but the logic of that analysis would almost lead to the assumption that when the palette is spread with color it accounts for the masterpiece.

   In my own retrospective meditation, I could discover often the elements later fused into poetry without this to me lessening the mystery. I remember reading about forty years ago a criticism of Hegel's philosophy of the Absolute becoming self-conscious in the unfolding of the universe. The writer's objection was that no change could take place in that which was already absolute and perfect, but that it might be said of the divine mind in its going forth through nature. I do not know why this logic remained in memory. A little later I found some Indian mystic correlating divine mind with primordial substance. In my own imagination, I had thought of primordial substance as the mirror of that Mind and therefore the Ancient Beauty. So were assembled in my mind before the birth of a poem the ideas implicit in it. But when the poem was born it was as much a surprise to me as if a flower had suddenly glowed before me in the hollow of air.

> Its edges foamed with amethyst and rose,
> Withers once more the old blue flower of day.
> There where the aether like a diamond glows
> Its petals fade away.
>
> A shadowy tumult stirs the dusky air:
> Sparkle the delicate dews, the distant snows;
> The great deep thrills, for through it everywhere
> The breath of Beauty blows.
>
> I saw how all the trembling ages past,
> Moulded to her by deep and deeper breath,
> Near to the hour when Beauty breathes her last
> And knows herself in death.

The verses came to me almost as swift as thought one evening while I was sitting on some rocks. There was no preconsciousness of the idea before I began to murmur line after line. I was unconscious of creation. It is true that antecedent to the poem there were certain ideas gathered months before, but not at all in memory when the poem came to me. The ideas were there as colors might lie on a palette, but the artist who blended them and who made the design was behind the consciousness which received the words. Whatever went to making an intricate harmony of color and sound—the imagination of the ending of the long tale of time, of nature become so ethereal that it was the perfect mirror of deity, and the withdrawal of the universe into the Pleroma—all that was wrought in some secret laboratory within the psyche. I remember my own delighted surprise when a line came,

Withers once more the old blue flower of day,

as if it had been read in the song of another poet. I can only assume that the philosophical antecedents in some way followed the psyche into that high state where, as the seers tell us, the gold-gleaming genius makes beauty, joys, rejoicings, dance, and song, and it changed the dry-as-dust logic into color and music and a rapture of prophecy.

I do not know in the ascension to the spiritual of our earth-born ideas as they reach the immortal whether they break out in a glory of words, a glory of images, or a glory of thought, or whether these coexist in a glory of being. What comes back to us from that high sphere loses beauty in its descent, as Ishtar in the Chaldean myth had crown and scepter and the royalty of her robes taken from her when descending from heaven to earth.

I know that there is loss, for once consciousness was kindled in me in the deep of sleep. I was in some profundity of being. There was neither sight nor sound, but all was a motion in deep being. Struggling desperately to remain there, I was being dragged down to the waking state, and then what was originally a motion in deep being broke into a dazzle of images which symbolized in some dramatic way the motion of life in that profundity. And still being drawn down there came a third state in which what was originally deep own-being, and after that images, was later translated into words. This experience I told to Yeats, who said he had an identical experience of the three states. But even what I remembered of this threefold change may itself have been but remembered symbolic dream. But I surmise that whatever faint relation to divine being there may be in our waking thought, as it ascends to the fourth state of spirit-illumination, the germinal idea is perfected. From the segment the circle is completed, and its perfection is the mirroring in the psyche of the archetype of the idea in the divine mind. Here we only receive frail echoes in words which do not hold at all or only a faint trace of the pristine and magical beauty, as in a muddy street may shine faintly in its wetness the reflection of a star.

I discovered too that when the waking consciousness imagined it had found matter for fine poetry in something heard or read, and it tried to shape the idea into poetical form, it often received no aid from the genie within. The Indian sages say the spirit is not taken by thought. It takes whom it wills. By this I understand that wisdom in such matters comes from within. The idea brings itself to birth.

I once read a fragment quoted from the Vaishnava scriptures about the childhood of Krishna; how he ran on all fours over the household, yet the sages spoke of him as the Ancient and Unborn; how he played with the milkmaids, yet he was called the Purest of the Pure and the most ascetic of sages allowed the claim. From this I turned away with the outer mind and I tried to imagine a poem of lovers in the Indian forest, where men and maidens went past the body and saw within each other god and goddess, Radha and Krishna. But the poem would not write itself. Then the psyche some years after projected into the waking consciousness its own transfiguration of the fragment, completing the cycle of life from birth to death, in which there is always the mystery of fallen life and unfallen majesty together in the same being.

I paused beside the cabin door and saw the King of
    Kings at play,

Tumbled upon the grass I spied the little heavenly
    runaway.

The mother laughed upon the child made gay by
    its ecstatic morn,

But yet the sages spake of It as of the Ancient and
    Unborn.

I heard the passion breathed amid the
    honeysuckle-scented glade,

And saw the King pass lightly from the beauty
    that He had betrayed.

I saw him change from love to love. But yet the
    pure allowed His claim

To be the purest of the pure, thrice holy, stainless,
    without blame.

I saw the open tavern-door flash on the dusk a
    ruddy glare,

And saw the King of Kings outcast reel brawling
    through the starlit air.

But yet He is the Prince of Peace of whom the
    ancient wisdom tells,

And by their silence men adore the lovely silence
    where He dwells.

I saw the King of Kings again, a thing to shudder at
    and fear,

A form so darkened and so marred that childhood
    fled if it drew near.

And yet He is the Light of Lights whose blossoming
    is Paradise,

That Beauty of the King which dawns before the
    seer's enraptured eyes.

I saw the King of Kings again, a miser with a heart
    grown cold;

And yet He is the Prodigal, the Spendthrift of the
Heavenly Gold,

The largesse of whose glory crowns the blazing
brows of cherubim,

And sun and moon and starry fires are jewels
scattered forth by Him.

I saw the King of Kings descend the narrow door-
way to the dust

With all his fires of morning still, the beauty,
bravery and lust.

And yet He is the life within the Ever-living
Living Ones,

The Ancient with Eternal Youth, the cradle of the
infant suns,

The fiery fountain of the stars, and He the golden
urn where all

The glittering spray of planets in their myriad
beauty fall.

I had always the sense of a will above my own, and if
I turned from it I had no inspiration. My friend Yeats
believes poetry to be fashioned more by the conscious
mind, but how could he choose so perfectly among words
if there were not a perfection of which he was unconscious
which was within him to guide his choice? I did find as I
grew older that I had a more conscious art in verse-
making, as if the psyche had found a place in the waking
mind and there was less of a dramatic sundering between
the creative and the receiving consciousness. A poem like
that from which I quoted my interpretation of the
Upanishadic teaching about the phases of sleep seemed to
me the outcome of the external mind grown to some
maturity of its own, and able to act and think from its own
center, whereas when I was young I had little but intuition.
In my age, too, I think I shape poetry more out of my

experience of life, as in the poem *Germinal* in the first chapter of this book.

The things I did when I was younger have been brooded over, and something of the brooding has gone inward to the realm of the Interpreter and been returned with some wisdom of the Interpreter added to it. But though the later poems appear to be more the product of the conscious waking mind, I am not sure that I am not deceived about this, and they may be as much born in the deeps of being as the earlier verses which came like words whispered from another nature. I do not know whether I am still receiving oracles out of the psyche, or whether I am not like that sad singer lost in the Caves of Lilith, playing with symbols left in a temple from which the divinity had departed, where the ancient ritual is still sung but in the absence of the indwelling god.

8

I AM a far exile from that great glory which inhabits the universe, and can but peer through some momentary dusky transparency in my nature to a greater light than the light of day. I know the royal road is by practice of the great virtues. But I cannot speak that language or urge those obligations, I who have been angry and sensual. I can only speak where I have been faithful. I have never ceased from the inward search, and might by that faithfulness have gone far if I had not a rabble of desires tugging me by the skirts to travel alluring roads in the world of illusion. I could peer only a little way, apprehending behind form the Creator, behind thought the Thinker, behind intuition the Seer, behind conscience the Love, and in fallen life some still unfallen majesty, and even in the basest desires could find signs of their spiritual ancestry.

> There was never sin of thine
> But within its heart did dwell
> A beauty that could whisper thee
> Of the high heaven from which it fell.

I tell what I have surmised or discovered, by reason perhaps of that uncorrupted spiritual atom in my nature.

I know there must be error even in our highest approaches to the true if the whole nature has not been purified and made transparent. Emanations from our dark untransmuted desires must discolor our vision. The deepest things in my life came to me in the form of poetry, and I brooded upon every circumstance in its uprising that I might discover its ancestral fountain. However slight may be the song contrasted with the great poetry of the world, it was as high above my normal mood as that great poetry is above mine. I could not but wonder at it, for at times there was some magic in its coming which seemed almost to dissolve the personality. A music would be born in the deeps of being which could not get completely incarnated in the words, but which swept them together until they were not at all like the stumbling, almost inarticulate, speech of the boy. I remember as if yesterday that day in my youth when a mystical music was born in me before ever thought came or the words that followed.

> When the breath of twilight blows to flame the
>   misty skies,
> All its vaporous sapphire, violet glow and silver
>   gleam,
> With their magic flood me through the gateway
>   of the eyes.
> I am one with the twilight's dream.
>
> When the trees and skies and fields are one in their
>   dusky mood
> Every heart of man is rapt within the mother's
>   breast.
> Full of peace and sleep and dream in the vasty
>   quietude,
> I am one with their hearts at rest.
>
> From our immemorial joys of hearth and home and love,
> Strayed away along the margin of the unknown tide,

All its reach of soundless calm can thrill me far above
Words or touch from the lips beside.

Aye, and deep and deep and deeper let me drink and
    draw
From the olden fountain more than light or peace or
    dream;
Such primaeval being as o'erfills the heart with awe
Growing one with its silent stream.

By the magic of that music which so rose within me
the universe seemed to reel away from me, and to be
remote and unsubstantial as the most distant nebulae,
and for some minutes I was able to re-create within myself
the musical movement of the power, and could stay the
soul upon the high uplands. But it quickly vanished as a
dream might go after our waking, and try as I might I could
not recall it again. But for a moment I understood what
power might be in sound or incantation. It made me
understand a little those mystics who speak of travelling
up a Jacob's Ladder of Sound to the Logos, the fountain
of all melody.

I found later if meditation on the Spirit is prolonged
and profound enough we enter on a state where our being
is musical, not a music heard without but felt within as if
the soul itself had become music, or had drawn nigh to the
ray of the Logos, the Master Singer, and was for that
instant part of its multitudinous song. While *By the
Margin of the Great Deep* was being conceived I felt that
music in my being before the words were swept together,
a state akin to that I experienced waking in dream when
I followed in their descending order the phases from deep
own-being through images or symbols to their last echo in
words. I held these memories with others akin to them,
hoping that at last I might understand the psyche and

come to some mastery of the hidden powers.

I do not think we shall ever come to truth otherwise than by such gropings in the cave of the soul, when with shut eyes we are in a dim illuminated darkness, and seek through transient transparencies to peer into the profundities of being. It is the most exciting of all adventures, the exploration of the psyche, even though the windows out of which we gaze are soon darkened for us by our own bodily emanations. Yet there are enchanted moments when we have vision, however distant, of the divinities who uphold the universe. It is true we are at an immense distance from their greatness, and see them as a shepherd boy far away among his hills might see the glittering of the army of a great king, and he is awed by the majesty and bows low at the vision of greatness, and dreams over it when the army is past and he turns to his humble task with his sheep. So remotely is it I have apprehended splendors overshadowing my insignificance. They stand over all of us. I think if we chose the least inspiring among those we know, one seeming not at all puissant or entitled to respect, and could know of the immortal powers which uphold the frailty of his being, his darkened life would seem to the imagination to move in a blaze of glory.

There are many who would speak lightly of the serious mood in which I pondered over the songs which I think of as oracles out of the psyche. Yet they themselves may pay reverence to the voices of conscience or of intuition which also are oracles out of undiscovered depths in their own being, and intuition and conscience may utter themselves in song as well as in fugitive illuminations of mind, heart, or will. My meditations were all intent on the discovery of the nature of soul and spirit. I write now in age, remembering indeed the circumstance about the writing of poetry, but there is some blurring of intensity and keenness of mind, and I cannot re-create the old intensity of emotion or thought.

No sooner does there come illumination than it is gone. I cannot stay it for an instant. Time inexorably hurries us from the god who dies away in hazes of memory, hurries us from exultation, exquisite ardors, emotions, and anguish, and from the dead with whom we had willingly died so that we might go hand in hand with them into the darkness.

I have deferred too long this work, for I can no more evoke the magic of moods that might have brought with me those who read, and I would not have been so frail a guide for them in the labyrinths of being. But as we near the end of our stay here, knowing we must soon start on other travelling, we begin thought on what we would take with us. In our last meditations, we gather together in soul what was most precious to pay for a habitation in the country in which we shall be newcomers. The seers who had known not only life but death said that what we think of last here is the starting-point of life in that other world, and that death is the beginning of a long meditation in which soul returns to spirit, the Son to the Father, as a prince who has led armies goes back to his king with the spoils of conquest. As we travel inward from time to the Ever-living we shall, if our thought be set on that and not on the desires of the body, regain what had passed from us here.

As I get older, my poetry seems to be less revelation out of the psyche than the summing up of whatever wisdom the outer mind had gathered. But almost the last poem which seemed to me to come out of the genie in the innermost with the old authenticity made promise that no precious thing would be lost, and when we went inward to our own immortal we would regain all that Time had taken away.

Be not so desolate
Because thy dreams have flown,
And the hall of the heart is empty
And silent as stone,
As age left by children
Sad and alone.

Those delicate children,
Thy dreams, still endure.
All pure and lovely things
Wend to the Pure.
Sigh not. Unto the fold
Their way was sure.

Thy gentlest dreams, thy frailest,
Even those that were
Born and lost in a heart-beat,
Shall meet thee there.
They are become immortal
In shining air.

The unattainable beauty,
The thought of which was pain,
That flickered in eyes and on lips
And vanished again;
That fugitive beauty
Thou shalt attain.

Those lights innumerable
That led thee on and on,
The masque of time ended,
Shall glow into one.
They shall be with thee for ever,
Thy travel done.

9

I THINK all true poetry was conceived on the Mount of Transfiguration and there is revelation in it and the mingling of heaven and earth. The Mount is a symbol for that peak of soul when, gone inward into itself, it draws nigh to its own divine root, and memory and imagination are shot through and through with the radiance of another nature. It is not alone poetry definitely mystical which is so conceived. The romantic imagination, equally with the mystical, released from the clog of our slower, more static nature, blossoms into its own ideal. There the imagination might move with the wizard airy glow of the *Ancient Mariner* or *Kubla Khan*, or have the stained glass richness of the *Eve of St. Agnes*, or the heart-choking sweetness of Shelley's music, or the phantom beauty of *Usheen* in Tirnanoge, or build itself a *Palace of Art* with exquisite enamelings on its cloud-built chambers. Whatever is germinal here finds there its perfection and culmination. Our inspiration will be as our aspiration. A seer in the Upanishads said of the seeker:

Let him approach it saying, "This is the Mighty."
He becomes mighty. Let him approach it saying,
"This is the Wise." He becomes filled with wisdom.
Let him approach it saying, "This is the Maker of
    the Song." He becomes the Maker of the Song.

There are many who are not consciously mystical but
who do yet before they sleep rest on and confide to some
dweller in the innermost their problems, having found
that what was obscure often became clear on their waking.
Some healers I have known refer their doubts about a
diagnosis to this wisdom which has never been to the
schools. From this being comes the revealing flash to the
scientist, the intuition about law or the movement of
forces; and knowledge might rightly come from a ray of
that Mind which is Shepherd over the vast horde of
elements and powers, for the maker of the law needs no
mechanism to discover the law.

I do not know of any psychology which so spiritually
excites me as this of the nightly return of the soul to the
divine order, that we who through the day are absorbed in
petty labors do go back to an unfallen nature, unto our
own high magnificence, and are in council with the
Cosmocratores. Our Eden is not left behind time, but is all
about us and within us, a paradise to be regained as we
regain the innocence of wisdom. Many a time has this
thought comforted me in fetid slum and murky alley where
the devil hath his many mansions. Passing through these
I would remember the peaks reached in meditation, and
the wisdom of the seers who taught that all these creatures
slip away from their wretchedness, from that diabolical
riot to the ancient beauty. For every one of these wretched
were spoken the comforting words of the Ancestral Self, "I
will not leave thee or forsake thee," and again of all these

it was written, "Their angels do always behold the face of the Father."

> By many a dream of God and man my thoughts in
>   shining flocks were led,
> But as I went through Patrick Street the hopes and
>   prophecies were dead.
> The hopes and prophecies were dead. They could not
>   blossom where the feet
> Walked amid rottenness nor where the brawling
>   shouters stamped the street.
> Where was the beauty that the Lord gave men when
>   first they towered in pride?
> But one came by me at whose word the bitter
>   condemnation died.
> His brows were crowned with thorns of light. His eyes
>   were bright as one who sees
> The starry palaces shine o'er the sparkle of the
>   heavenly seas.
> "Is it not beautiful?" He cried, "Our Fairyland
>   of Heart's Desire
> Is mingled through the mire and mist, yet stainless
>   keeps its lovely fire.
> The pearly children with blown hair are dancing
>   where the drunkards reel:
> The cloud-frail daffodils shine out where filth is
>   splashing from the heel.
> O sweet and sweet and sweet to hear, the melodies
>   in rivers run.
> The rapture of their crowded notes is yet the
>   myriad voice of One.
> Those who are lost and fallen here to-night in sleep
>   shall pass the gate,
> Put on the purples of the King and know them
>   masters of their fate.

Each wrinkled hag shall reassume the blooms and
  hues of Paradise,
Each brawler be enthroned in calm among the
  children of the Wise.
Yet in the council with the gods no one will falter
  to pursue
His lofty purpose but come forth the cyclic labours
  to renew,
And take the burden of the world and dim his beauty
  in a shroud
And wrestle with the chaos till the Anarch to the
  light be bowed.
We cannot for forgetfulness forgo the reverence
  due to them
Who wear at times they do not guess the sceptre and
  the diadem.
As bright a crown as thus was theirs when first they
  from the Father sped.
Yet look with deeper eyes and still the ancient
  beauty is not dead."
He mingled with the multitude. I saw their brows
  were crowned and bright,
A light about the shadowy heads, a shadow
  round the brows of light.

It is implied in this that we came to this world by our
own will and for some purpose, and this thought has been
with me since I was a boy, when I broke out in a fierce revolt
at the idea that I was born into this world not by my own
will and would be punished if I neglected to do what I had
never undertaken to do. I remember the deep peace which
came to me when I had the intuition that Christ, Pro-
metheus, are in every heart, that we all took upon ourselves
the burden of the world like the Christ, and were foreseers
as Prometheus was of the agony of the labor he undertook,

until the chaos is subdued and wrought in some likeness to the image in the divine imagination.

It will be seen that I look on the poet as prophet. I think, indeed, that almost the only oracles which have been delivered to humanity for centuries have come through the poets, though too often they have not kept faith with the invisible and have been guilty of the sin of simony. But at times they still receive the oracles, as did the sybils of old, because in the practice of their art they preserve the ancient tradition of inspiration and they wait for it with airy uplifted mind. They know, as Corot knew about painting, that you must go a little beyond yourself, and whatever revelation of beauty, of the spirit, has been in Europe for many centuries has come, not from the Churches, who hold they already have truth, but from the poets who are still the seekers, and who at times have that lordly utterance as if the God were speaking through His prophets.

Let no one assume that I claim for even their highest utterance that infallibility which those who do not desire to think ask from their teachers, but it is through the poets and musicians alone that we get the sense of a glory transmitted from another nature, and as we mingle our imagination with theirs we are exalted and have the heartache of infinite desire. Truth for us cannot be in statements of ultimates but in an uplifting of our being, in which we are raised above ourselves and know that we are knocking at the door of the Household of Light. The poets and the great masters of music are those who have the expectation of inspiration. They wait upon the gods though they may not know when they turn inward in reverie what being it is upon whom they wait. They receive according to the quality of their desire. It may be with one but a momentary glow, an inner music imposed upon the words they use, a heartache in lovely distances, a tenderness dropping through the air, a love breathed upward through the dark clay, a beauty born out of suffering, or a blinding revelation. But the oracle has in it some magic of a higher nature woven into music so that it can be remembered and may re-create the wonder out of which it was born.

It is probable that the bad hexameters in which the Oracles of Apollo were delivered in the decadence of the mysteries continued the tradition of a time when the Earth-born waited on the Heaven-born in a rapt awe and the immortals uttered their oracles, a divine speech, through the purity of prophet or priest. No Church today can convince me that it is inspired until the words arising from it even in anger break in a storm of beauty on the ear.

10

I HAVE been exploring so far as I might into the psyche and the worlds it moves in, and its action upon waking consciousness. I had vivid memories of the projection of dream stories from inner to outer, of waking and finding words rushing out of dream into waking, of what seemed to me transient intersectings of the circle of my own being with the lives of others brought about by some spiritual affinity. I have told something of these.

About a large part of the verse I wrote I have no such vivid memories, for the fusion between inner and outer was too swift, and I could not get evidence of the duality between creator and recipient which I surmised. If I had not these other memories, I might have thought there was nothing in poetry more than an intensity of waking imagination. But in that retrospective meditation I found things which were curious, a guidance from within in regard to my intellectual interests. I had begun after I was thirty or thereabouts to evolve a quick superficial intelligence, interests in art, economics, and politics, and the ideas which excited my own generation. It was that quickness of mind which enabled me a little later to live as a critic of politics, economics, and literature. I never found conscience or intuition staying my mind when I engaged in these necessary duties. But if I thought of using imagination apart from these obligations, to draw upon the psyche to aid me in works of imagination other than mystical poetry or mystical prose, I would find no inspiration. I could imagine easily original plots for stories or plays, but never received any impulse to write them. I had no glow of excitement at the thought of writing a great story or a great play. It was not my Dharma, as the Indians would say.

Everyone in their philosophy has some particular work to do, and to desert that and attempt the work of others, however estimable, is full of danger. Everything of which I had inner approval was related to the search for the spirit, and when I would bend my mind upon other things, try for instance to plan out a long tale, I would find myself led back to my own center. Imagination would move as a bubble under water which is for ever seeking to rise to its native air. It may be delayed under rock or waterweed, but it slips ever upward until at last it comes to the surface.

I remember I once planned out a tale about a novelist who had gone into the country to write a long story. There were two characters, a man and a woman, who had begun to live with a vivid actuality in his mind. He could see them moving about and he knew what was in their thoughts. It was their custom in the evening to walk along a ridge of rock which ran out into the sea. They would sit there and talk. The man had a rich vitality and many ambitions, but the whole life of the girl was rooted in that country of mountains, lakes, and sea. There was love but some sundering of ideals between these twain. While the story-teller was putting his imagination into words, he was visited by a friend who enquired about his work. He told him a little about the two characters he had imagined, and his friend cried out, "But I know two people exactly like that," and he went on talking about them. As he talked the story-teller suddenly realized that what he thought was pure imagination was really a vision of life, for his friend had told him things about the man and woman which he had already known and written down. He said nothing, but, when his friend had gone, he surrendered himself more and more to his imagination about the two. The artist in him demanded a rather tragic end of the spiritual conflict.

Some months later the story-teller's friend visited him again, and the story-teller asked him about those two who were so like his imagined characters. The friend told him about a trouble which had risen between them, and the story-teller suddenly realized that his own powerful imagination had been molding their actions toward a tragic end. And in my imaginary tale the story-teller in a panic went a long journey to break in upon the man and girl and tell them what havoc he had been making of their love, and it was he and not they themselves who had brought them to this tragic sundering of their lives.

When I had imagined so far, I lost interest in the tale and the man. I began to think of that mystical girl, and could see her alone and without any unhappiness, not with that lover but with a thousand loves. And the moment I saw her so, the bubble of the spiritual imagination, which had been hindered on its way to light by that cloud of circumstance, slipped from beneath the last obstruction, and a poem which seemed have been waiting for a mood in which it could incarnate began at once to sing itself in my mind.

A myriad loves
Her heart would confess
That thought but one
To be wantonness.

And this was why
She could not stay,
From the gilded fireside
Running away,

To be on the hillside,
Gay and alone,
A twilight Sibyl
With rock for her throne.

There she was sweetheart
To magical things,
To cloudland, woodland,
Mountains and springs.

She yielded to them,
But was not the less
Pure, but the more,
For that wantonness.

For through these lovers
Her spirit grew
To be clear as crystal
And cool as dew.

Their bridal gift
Was to make her be
Initiate
Of their company;

To know the lovely
Voices of these,

Of light, of earth,
Of wind and of trees,

Whose wisdom flowed
From a fullness, yea,
From bygone ages
And far away.

So thronged was her spirit
It seemed a pack
That carried the moon
And stars on her back.

When the spirit wakens
It will not have less
Than the whole of life
For its tenderness.

And that was why
She could not stay,
From the gilded fireside
Running away.

She laughed in herself
On her seat of stone.
"It would be wanton
To love but one."

I could tell many tales of what at first seemed a
wandering of the imagination, but from which I was finally
led back to my destiny as mystical poet. I felt as if there
were a shepherd within who brought back the flock of
strayed desires and fancies to a fold which was their own.
Even in my economic studies which led me to write *The
National Being* I was brought to think less of circumstance
than of the spirit behind national movements, and from
that I was brought to the more completely mystical mood

of *The Interpreters*, where the politic of the characters is traced back to motions in Anima Mundi. However I might wander in imagination, misled by desires, fantasy, or ambition, an uneasy undercurrent set in, and I was guided back to the path from which I had so often strayed. I came at last almost to believe that, like Ulysses in the Platonic myth, I had chosen before birth a life in which I was primarily to be mystic, and I could not conflict with that primal will without finding many of the inhabitants of the soul deserting me. It is not merely in moral crises that interior guidance begins to manifest as conscience. There is not a moment in life, not the least action or thought, where the spiritual law if supplicated is not ready to declare itself.

Do I build too much upon too slight foundations? But do we not all in life follow the faintest stars which flicker in the gloom of being? Do we not really trust these faint lights of intuition, because they are lights, more than reason, which is often too slow a counselor for us to resort to? They may seem to mislead us, those lights, but one never went out before another and brighter light had glowed to lead us out of that cave of the body in which we are confined. Life and feeling are too swift runners for us to run alongside them unless we have as guide a pacemaker, intuition, which is swift as any.

11

I HAD found the genie in the innermost sometimes overcoming me by an enchantment of dream flooding the waking consciousness, not merely when I was meditative, but when I was at other work or walking in the streets or on country roads. At other times I found the poem or the idea of a poem rushing directly on me out of sleep as if it were an outcast from light. Again I found the inspiration for poetry in what I believe was a momentary fusion of my own being with the souls of others brought into a psychic intimacy by some affinity of emotion or thought.

I have now to tell how a symbolic vision or dream was projected into the waking consciousness while I was engaged in meditation. In this meditation, when I had closed my eyes, the psyche became like one of those crypts of the mysteries where, as the ancients relate, they saw images of gods and immortals in a clear, immovable, and blessed light. But what I first saw was not a clear light, but the darkness of the cave, that cloudy gloom we peer into when we shut out the light of this world. Then the gloom began to become alive with moving forms. I was looking into an immense chamber in which huge misshapen beings, part monster animal, part giant man, moved restlessly. The only clear light in that darkness was a kind of fiery twilight glittering with stars, the gleaming from a golden throne at the far end of that chamber, a light, it seemed, caught from a last inflammation in the sky which came through a gigantic doorway facing the throne. On this throne sat one who seemed to be King, a being of a higher order than those misshapen creatures who prowled about the hall. There was a dim radiance about his head. He seemed sunken in melancholy, oblivious of the monsters sprawling before him. Beside the King, with a hand upon the throne, was a slender beautiful girl. Then my own understanding was quickened, for the genie in the innermost who projected these images before the inner eye had flooded the mind with understanding, and I knew at once this King was Nuada of the Silver Hand, who was King of the Tuatha De Danann when they were overcome by the dark Fomorian powers.

Some time before this I had been reading ancient Irish saga, and one scholar had found something which linked Nuada to a Norse divinity, a god who sacrificed himself. I had said to myself, "Nuada may be the Prometheus of the ancient Irish." My interpretation of the vision was that I had gone asleep and had carried this speculation into the psyche and up to that higher state of soul where the imagination "goes forth," to use Blake's phrase, "in its uncurbed glory." And it had imagined in completeness a vast myth. When later I began my nightly meditation, I was met in the mid-world by these images projected from the Mount of Transfiguration. The dream-pictures had a swift movement and as swift an interpretation. I knew as I looked on these images that Nuada was the heroic heaven-descended will, and he had come with other divine companions to earth to conquer it and bring wisdom to its dark inhabitants. But the brightness of the immortals had been obscured by a sorcery breathing out of earth. These monstrous shapes were earth-born passions and desires which had enslaved the incarnate divinity. The divine powers had on earth been turned to infernal uses. Angus, the Celtic Eros, was singing love songs for the Fomorians. Diancecht, the god physician, had become healer of their loathsome diseases. Dana clothed their terrible desires with beauty. Ogma, the champion, taught them the arts of war. Only Nuada remembered the heroic thought which had brought himself and his companions from heaven to earth.

Sometimes in this mythological vision there would be images. Then these would disappear and the mind would comprehend swiftly the meanings, leaping the void between one series of images and another.

I knew that slender lovely woman was Armid, and she was asking Nuada to tell the story which he alone remembered, for the immortals had passed away from themselves and had forgotten all. Then the high King told her the story of the gods from the dawn of time when the divine world was fashioned, and how its dark image, the underworld, came into being, and how at last the peace of the divine world was shattered by the anguish in the underworld, for sorrow had grown to be more powerful than joy. Then Nuada had summoned the immortals to a great adventure of conquest and healing. All the immortals promised aid. They descended the ladder of the spheres and came at last to earth where they were at first welcomed, but were at last overcome by its sorcery; and now the immortals only held sway over its dark inhabitants when by their arts, out of the glory still within them, they made lovely to the Fomorians their own bestial desires.

After the first vision of the great palace of the King, the images faded and there came the swift leaping of the mind in interpretation. Then the images broke in again on the trembling screen of the interior light, for Armid—frightened by the hoggish lust of one of the Fomorians, and shivering through all her body—fled from the hall through the great door, and raced blindly on and on until the cold waters stayed her, and she paused, holding her heart that fluttered like a bird at the long peril of the night in time. She grew still at last pacing to and fro by the sea.

Then a light came from the west as if the sunken sun was re-arising. It grew greater coming swiftly across the waters, sending long lanes of fire before it. Out of that glory of light came a great flame-colored warrior on a winged steed. It was Lug, the sun god, riding out of the Land of Promise.

Then the images faded again, and for the first time my thought followed the ancient saga where Lug sent by the door-keeper a message to the High King that a champion had come to him out of the Land of Promise. Here the ancient story fitted itself into my dream. But when Lug entered the palace chamber the vision departed once more from the Saga, for the newcomer was invisible to all but the King.

Lug stood beside Nuada and told him to command the Fomorians to be still. The hall became silent, for when the King willed the Fomorians must obey. Then Lug told the King that he, Nuada, the power that was will, alone was real, that Angus, Ogma, Dana, Diancecht, and the rest were but phantom images of the immortals, the shadows of love, beauty, or thought; and, by the power of Lug, the

King was lifted above himself to his ancient divinity, and he saw all about him the true immortals, each speaking to him out of their own high ecstasy. They made promises to be truly with him at his labors until the great battle of Moytura to be fought at the end of time. The immortals then vanished and Nuada was left once more brooding in the great chamber, and the Fomorians there again began their restless prowling.

The vision seemed to me to be like one of those sacred mysteries enacted in crypt or sanctuary where those who had been purified could see in a mystic light the images of gods and immortals, that glass of which Saint Paul, who uses often the language of the mystery cults, spoke saying, "we see now in the glass darkly." I knew that such things could be, for once in my youth there came a visitor to our city who made clear my inner sight, and he showed me in that glass of aether images of magical things, of mystery celebrations and the unfolding of the wings of the psyche from the husk of the body, and of the return of the Son to the bosom of the Father, all as if enacted by radiant figures in that mystic light.

This projection of a myth about Nuada of the Silver Hand I understood to be an invitation to me to write what I saw or understood in a long narrative poem, and I was moved to write a thousand lines or more. But my talent was lyrical and ran only to brief intensities. I was deflected, too, by my labors in this world, where I was sent here and there to organize farmers, and I could not maintain any high exaltation or continuity of mood. The mystical narrative was dropped and I only printed one fragment of what I had written. This was the voice of Dana speaking to Nuada revealing the true nature of the Mighty Mother, the goddess, not of earthly love, but of a divine tenderness and pity.

I am the tender voice calling away,
Whispering between the beatings of the heart,
And inaccessible in dewy eyes
I dwell, and all unkissed on lovely lips,
Lingering between white breasts inviolate,
And fleeting ever from the passionate touch,
I shine afar till men may not divine
Whether it is the stars or the beloved
They follow with rapt spirit. And I weave
My spells at evening, folding with dim caress,
Aerial arms and twilight dropping hair,
The lonely wanderer by wood or shore,
Till, filled with some vast tenderness he yields,
Feeling in dreams for the dear mother heart
He knew ere he forsook the starry way,
And clings there, pillowed far above the smoke
And the dim murmur from the duns of men.
I can enchant the trees and rocks, and fill
The dumb brown lips of earth with mystery,
Make them reveal or hide the God, myself
Mother of all, but without hands to heal,
Too vast and vague, they know me not, but yet
I am the heartbreak over fallen things,
The sudden gentleness that stays the blow,
And I am in the kiss that foemen give
Pausing in battle, and in the tears that fall
Over the vanquished foe, and in the highest,
Among the Danaan gods, I am the last
Council of mercy in their hearts where they
Mete justice from a thousand starry thrones.
My heart shall be in thine when thine forgives.

I have condemned myself many times for my lack of
persistence and of faith that the genie in the innermost

would have given inspiration to complete a narrative which I thought needed too lordly a style for my talent. The symbolic interpretation of the ancient story was projected into my mind when I was intent on meditation. It was the vastest of any imaginations I had. I had the sense while it was present to consciousness that it was a symbolic message which I was to interpret and retell. But I failed in this as in so many other things, never having confidence in my own powers until I grew old and began to receive praise at a time when the powers were going inward from a body which was no longer tremulously sensitive and could not melt at an idea, and the psyche had almost lost its free gay movement in the upper airs.

There are many who have symbolic dreams, and if they brooded on them I am sure they would come to have faith in that dweller in the innermost. As they see images in the inner light, they may come to understand how in the mysteries—to those who were purified—the Wise Ones could on that clear and blessed light bring images of their inner selves, of gods and immortals, before them, so that they might know something of their own yet unveiled magnificence and "to feel that they are greater than they know."

12

THE high noon of time is past. We are nearing to its twilight, but are like children who run about and play and do not hear the voices calling them homewards, though indeed they are weary and their play has not in it the young delight of their dawn. How may we start on this travel? The scriptures, which are the high Oracles of the Oversoul, have told us the way. But they speak a language so high that few can understand its symbolism, for it is to most of us like a speech maintained in the court of a great king— an ancient aristocratic speech—while the rabble without think, chatter, and barter with each other in a vulgar tongue from which courtesy, dignity, and beauty are absent. I cannot speak that high language of the seers who wrote the scriptures of the world. I am as a child puzzled and enchanted by the wood into which he has strayed, who has the feeling that there is One who is playing hide-and-seek with it in the tangle, and the child peers through the leaves for a presence which always eludes it. I have never had the high vision of those who have gone into the deeps of being and who have returned rapture-blinded by the glory, and cried out in a divine intoxication to the Light of Lights:

Spread thy rays and gather them. The Light which is thy fairest form—I am what He is.

I am a far exile from that great glory, and can but peer through a dusky transparency to a greater light than the light of day. That greater light shines behind and through the psyche. It is the light of spirit which transcends the psyche as the psyche in its own world transcends the terrestrial ego. The psyche has a dual nature, for in part it is earth-bound, and in part it clings to the ancient spirit.

I do not think many have brooded long enough in that distinction of soul and spirit which Saint Paul made when writing to his friends at Corinth. He speaks of many unexplained things, of a third heaven, of soul and spirit, of psychic bodies and spiritual bodies, of a mysterious power which seems to be the fountain of all psychic powers, which enables one to discern spirits, and gives to another eloquence, speaking with tongues, poetry in fact, and to another magical or healing power. Some of these powers I tried to wake, but I will not here speak of them, for I am trying to supplicate the flame which gives wisdom rather than that which gives power.

While I could comprehend a little about the nature of the psyche, I could not apprehend at all the spirit which transcends the soul, for, as the seers said of it, it is eternal, invisible, and universal. Yet because it is universal we are haunted by it in every motion of mind. It is at the end of every way. It is present in sunlight. It nods at us from earth or air. As we pursue it, it ever eludes us, but it becomes more and more present until all that we see or are swims in a divine aether. I understand out of what emotion the Greek poet Aratus cried:

Full of Zeus are the cities. Full of Zeus are the harbours. Full of Zeus are all the ways of men;

for at times the familiar city in which I spent my life became strange to me, and its buildings, its ways, its lights and its darkness seemed but a magical movement in being. I did not know myself, nor did the dark crowds who went on their errands, but all, unknown to themselves, were on some secret mission which, when the multitudinous meditation was ended, would bring them to some divine consummation in the Great Deep or Holy Sepulchre.

That which is thought cannot grasp the thinker. The psyche is an entity, but what can we affirm of the spirit? We cannot say it is more within the heart than it is in air, or sunlight, rock, or sea, or that it is more in Heaven than Earth. It is within us and without us. When we love we are really seeking for it, and I think our most passionate kisses are given to that Lover who will not surrender to us. It cannot be constrained. But there are enchanted hours when it seems to be nigh us, nigher to us than the most exquisite sweetness in our transitory lives.

They tell in sacred story of those the spirit took to itself who had the infinite vision. I never came nigh that infinitude, but because I sought for it I was often happy and content knowing it was all about me. If I had stirred, it would have vanished. I never had other than a child's vision of the Father.

> I, with remembrance of our childhood only,
> Was stayed astonished at so vast a youth
> That bloomed suddenly through grey stones and air,
> Laughing, whirling, juggling its shining balls
> In their azure goblets, playing at hide-and-seek,
> An elf in the ivory delicate wild rose,
> Dilated in the zenith, sparkling afar,
> Here blurring the brown rough earth with beauty,
> Dancing to a grey beard as to a child.

O thou Ancient with Youth, dost thou see in me
The airy child who may so soon go forth?
Art thou the companion who shalt take my hand
In the dark valley? Wilt thou wear again
The shapes that were thy lovely hiding places
Where I found thee of old, secret in eyes,
Inviolate on lips, and in the heart unconquerable?
There was always for thee a door of escaping
Through which I could not follow. Even now
Tenderly frolic and intimate, if I would stay thee
Thou art gone inward, and thy light as lost
As the flying fishes, a pearly shadow that leaps
From the dark blue to slide in the dark blue.
As the high emperor I have never
Worshipped thee, making my dreams majestical
With thrones girt by the warriors of heaven,
My secret was thy gentleness. I know
No nurse had ever crooned a lullaby
So softly as thou the music that guides the loud
Tempest in its going forth. I know full well
When thou dancest into the heart that it may be
The rending of the heart. Yet the saints found
Clinging unto thee that their anguish burned
Upward to unimaginable delight.
I had not passion to press so to thee,
To know thee as the Mighty and the Wise.
But that I followed with so light a love
I was repaid, for every hour was filled
With a new changing beauty that was still
The ancient beauty. Here it glows on me
Within thy many-coloured garden, twilight,
A beauty that has never been before
Save for one silvery bloom, the Evening Star.

For that enchantment one needs no projection from the dream consciousness. It does not arise in dream. The spirit is with us even in the day, and I could not trace back to any artificer in the psyche the poetry which apprehends the presence here of the spirit. In my retrospective meditation, I noted that never in the dream consciousness had I any direct exalted sense of the presence of that spirit. In dream were beauty, imagination, desire, or terror, but all things in that mid-world of dream existed by way of fantasy or symbolism whether the dream was projected into the waking state or was experienced in sleep. While the dream consciousness flooded me I was mystic rather than spiritual: that is, true being was hidden under a mask. Out of the dream consciousness came beauty, but never under the influence of dream did I seem near to the spirit as when the exalted waking soul brooded upon the world.

I sometimes think the spirit is so with us here because the purpose of the highest is the conquest and transmutation of the lowest. The ancient seers warned us against the heavenworld and that it seduced by its sweetness and stayed us on our way to true being. Does the Divine deny its light to those who would go back to the heavens before they have fulfilled their labors here? I remember the promise of the god to Thrice-Great Hermes, if he followed the straight way, was not beauty in a heavenworld but an illumination in this world.

> It will everywhere meet thee and everywhere be seen of thee plain and easy, when thou dost not expect or look for it. It will meet thee waking, sleeping, sailing, travelling, by night, by day, when thou speakest or keepest silence. For there is nothing which is not the image of God.

It is, I sometimes think, in this world, not in another, that revelation will come and the purpose of incarnation be realized; and to come to our true wisdom we must think of Heaven and Hell as equally dragons in the path, both forms of the Maya which besets us and blinds the spiritual sight.

13

WHAT transformations may take place in our nightly travelling from our house of clay to the heaven of heavens. The seers who had gone into the highest being said that the soul in the profoundest deep of sleep touches on infinity.

I know nothing myself though I may surmise or imagine much. My farthest travelling inward was but a footstep. I would be overcome by a magic too mighty for me to hold back and would fall into the oblivion of slumber. But how many times when I meditated before sleeping did I not seem to myself to be sinking into light. How often when waking had I not the feeling that I had been cast forth and was rejected by heaven. Almost I looked for the waving of the flaming sword which nothing that is earthly can pass. I tried passionately from departing lights, fleeting visionary presences and intuition, to conjecture what wonders the soul may have known, with what beings it may have been in some high companionship.

Even in this world at times I had been aware of lordly beings. Once when I was young I had evoked the divine powers, supplicating their help in some work I was doing. I said to them, "I am trying to bring back your ancient reign," and I was answered, as I think, for as I was speaking later that night I, who was normally stuttering and stammering, suddenly felt as if I were thrust aside in my own body, and it was entered by some being who filled me with light, and I heard a voice speak through me to those about me, a voice like the voice Yeats spoke of,

the burning, live, unshaken voice
Of those who it may be can never die,

and I could see the amazed faces of those accustomed to my stumbling talk. After its aid was given that being departed from me, but left images and memories of its habitation in me, and all night long I was following up these flying traces and came at last to a vision of beings of flame in some place of wonder in Anima Mundi. At another time in my youth, when I was worn out, one of these beings leaned out of the air above me in my room, and from its hands came flaming emanations that poured on me and through me, and I was as one lifted from almost death to life, and felt for months after that a fiery invigoration of mind and body.

I have no doubt there are beings as far transcending us in wisdom and power as we may transcend the amoeba. In our journeyings inward to deep own-being, there may be grandiose transfigurations of the psyche and we may at last be partakers in divine mysteries. When Saint Paul spoke of being caught up to the third heaven, I believe he was in the same high plane of being the Indian seers spoke of. The genius in deep sleep they say may take many forms for himself as he comes to the sphere of creation. This high state we all enter, when we waken remembering not at all what we were or did, though we may have been changed inconceivably. Only the initiates into the highest mysteries could remember, and for them it might be as with Saint Paul that it was not lawful to speak of what was re-membered. For the rest there might be nothing at all remembered but some symbolic dream, or a vague psychic unrest or longing, or a fiery exaltation in the midst of their forgetfulness.

I sometimes think that the whole life of the soul, since it was first outbreathed by Deity, must be a struggle to find or re-create outside itself all that it first had within itself in the Pleroma. The soul fallen outside the divine circle begins to create in fantasy its lost infinitude. Something of the kind may take place in our microcosmic life when the soul wakens here. Its imaginations, philosophies, mysticism, its ardors and passions, may be symbols, echoes or images of its being in a higher state. To take an imagination which springs up in us, and to try to deduce from this what reality it mirrored, might seem almost as hopeless a task as for the non-mathematical mind to deduce what lies beneath formulae like the square root of minus one. Often I had an evidential emptiness about the reality behind my imaginations which might be mathematically symbolized by that formula, but yet something in me had flared out in a congregation of wild images which I contemplated with an intuition that what seemed so coherent within its own wildness must have some root in reality.

A Christian philosopher, considering what he called the extravagant speculations of the Gnostics, did yet say nobly of them, "We must remember that the mind of man is made in the image of God and therefore even in its wildest speculations it follows an image of truth." It is only that noble attitude of his I have to uphold me when I begin to consider another poem of my own. I had wakened from sleep with a rare exaltation, but had not even a dream to hint by its symbolism at what lay beneath that exaltation. Yet something in my forgetfulness was trying to create phantasmal images in poetry of some almost inconceivable adventure of the psyche. I do not know whether the imagination which was born in the waking consciousness had any relation to the being from which it had passed, but what follows was the outcome of that high exaltation, of the reason for which I knew nothing, for there was nothing in this world but ashes of some starry fires or dust of some heaven-assailing will.

> See, where the light streams over Connla's Fountain
> Starward aspire.
> The sacred sign upon the holy mountain
> Shines in white fire.
> Wavering and flaming yonder o'er the snows
> The diamond light
> Melts into silver, or to sapphire glows
> Night beyond night.
> And from the heaven of heavens descends on earth
> A dew divine.
> Come, let us mingle in the starry mirth
> About the shrine.
> O earth, enchantress, mother, to our home
> In thee we press,
> Thrilled by thy fiery breath and wrapt in some
> Vast tenderness.
> The homeward birds uncertain o'er their nest
> Wheel in the dome,
> Fraught with dim dreams of some enraptured rest,
> Another home.
> But gather ye to whose undarkened eyes

Night is as day.
Leap forth, immortals, birds of paradise,
In bright array.
Clothed as with shining tresses of the sun,
And by his name
Call from his haunt divine the ancient one,
Our Father Flame.
Aye, from the wonder light, heart of our star,
Come now, come now;
Sun-breathing spirit, ray thy lights afar.
Thy children bow,
Hush with more awe the heart. The bright-browed
   races
Are nothing worth
By those dread gods from out whose awful faces
The Earth looks forth
Infinite pity set in calm, whose vision cast
Adown the years
Beholds how beauty burns away at last
Their children's tears.
Now while our hearts the ancient quietness
Floods with its tide,
The things of air and fire and height no less
In it abide,
And, from their wandering over sea or shore,
They rise as one
Unto the vastness, and with us adore
The midnight sun,
And enter the innumerable All,
And shine like gold,
And starlike gleam in the immortals' hall,
The heavenly fold,
And drink the sun breaths from the Mother's lips
Awhile, and then

Fail from the light and drop in dark eclipse
To earth again,
Roaming along by heaven-hid promontory
Or valley dim,
Weaving a phantom image of the glory
They knew in Him.
Out of the fullness flow the winds. Their song
Is heard no more,
Or hardly breathes a mystic sound along
The dreamy shore.
Blindly they move, unknowing, as in trance,
Their wandering
Is half with us, and half an inner dance
Led by the King.

I had no memory of so high an adventure of the psyche, only a fire which seemed to have fallen out of heaven, and tried to re-create the intensity from which it had fallen, "weaving a phantom image of the glory." But it was so vivid that I was conquered by the fantasy and brooded on it as if it were revelation. The fantasy so created may not have had any more relation to truth than the relation Neander surmised lay in the vast mystical speculation of the Gnostics. A child as it grows up often carries a likeness to its parent, the germ out of which it came holding within itself somehow and unconsciously to itself an image of its begetter. In the same way the psyche, which in its own realm may have vision of infinite grandeurs, when it narrows itself to our clay may hold within itself some seed of its own high being, and in the house it builds for itself in the brain it may instinctively put forth symbolic images of its own primal magnificence.

It may be because of this the poets use at times a lordlier language than their contracted life here could justify. If not true to outward being, it may yet be true to inward or deep own-being. The fallen divinity for an instant forgets that it is fallen and speaks as to immortals.

There is as great a mystery about our least motion as there is about our whole being. We are affected by the whole cosmos. Emanations from most distant planets pour on us and through us. Everything is related to everything else. "Thou canst not stir a stone without troubling of a star." Let us still life to the utmost quietude, and what we feel in the stillness is pregnant as if there were multitudes in that intensity of loneliness. The universe seems involved in the simplest motion of mind. Just as the needle-point of a nerve in the eye is sensitive to light from the whole of the heavens spread above us, so at moments we feel that all knowledge is within us. But we have not yet evolved mind to be the perfect instrument to mirror universal mind as the eye mirrors infinitudes of light and darkness. But out of that center in us through which all the threads of the universe are drawn, there may come at times flashes of supernature; and by these flashes we live and hope and aspire, though nothing may remain when they go but some shadowy tale or vague exultant imagination like that poem about the mysteries I had written.

I feel what I have said about imagination to be very inadequate as portraiture. Even the simplest emotions need a more transcendental and complicated mathematic than the scientist devotes to the mysterious activity of the atom. How can words portray truly any emotion when the whole of life is involved in its parts, all the past, and, for all we know, the eternity we think of as the future?

To bring this loveliness to be
Even for an hour, the builder must

Have wrought in the laboratory
Of many a star for its sweet dust.

Oh, to make possible that heart,
And that gay breath so lightly sighed,
What agony was in the art,
How many gods were crucified!

Words can never be a perfect mirror for that complexity. But we must needs use them if only to have guidance to that point within us where the whole universe focuses its light on one fiery center.

14

"THE ONE became many," said the ancient seers. Every-thing therefore is divinely descended. Nothing came forth from that Majesty in which we may not discover some traces of its royal lineage. That is the excuse for the meditation on this book. Our lightest thoughts, our most fugitive ideas, do in obscure ways act and move by some magic like that which moves the universe.

With this idea in mind I have taken thoughts and fancies which, compared with the imaginations of the great masters, are of slight value, and have tried to track them a little nearer to their fountains. In this I was following as I could the wisdom of Socrates, where in *The Banquet* he speaks of a meditation which leads us into the mid-world of desires, thoughts, and imaginations. I was seeking the fountains of beauty and poetry, trying also to discover what I might of that Daimon or Genie who overshadows us and at times speaks through us.

I did not attain "a science equal to a beauty so vast": and I must often appear as one confused or bewildered in his thinking, or to be self-deceived. There is indeed a riotous fertility of fancy which at times chokes us and blinds us on our way to the True. When we would "explore the river of the soul whence or in what order we have come so that we may ascend whence we came," we are bewildered by imaginations like those elf-girls, each lovelier than the other, who in an Eastern tale try to allure the seeker from the Waters of Immortality. It is difficult to weed the garden of the soul from the quick springing up of the blossoms of illusion, for we have not plucked up one when another enchants us. We, by some magic, do make spiritual the images of earth so that feet which may only be whiteness of clay seem airy feet that might run along the clouds, and light limbs seem fashioned out of some burnished and exquisite air, and dawn and night ravished of colors and stars to make a beauty that glows pleroma-like. So over the images we see a glamour is cast, and if we succumb to it and clasp the image there is nothing left but fading fire or crumbling form.

Such a rabble of imaginations besets us that it is difficult to distinguish false from true, and we have little to guide us but intuition, which tells us to follow only those images which seem to have a lamp of spiritual meaning within them, which are not opaque but transparent, which do not stay us by their beauty, but suggest a lordlier beauty than their own. I think as we go inward images and ideas begin to glow as transparencies. They lead us beyond themselves and liberate us as Wordsworth does when he wrote:

Thy friends are exultations, agonies,

which illuminates our darkness like the angel who released Peter from prison. So in what I have written I told only of those imaginations which seemed to have a lamp of spiritual meaning within them. My own Daimon, in one of the earliest inspirations I had, warned me—

Oh, be not led away
Lured by the colour of the sun-rich day.

The gay romance of song
Unto the spirit life doth not belong.
Though far-between the hours
In which the Master of Angelic Powers
Lightens the dusk within
The holy of holies, be it thine to win
Rare vistas of white light . . .

and I have always feared to yield to beauty which had not that lamp. Yet I have not written this book to my satisfaction, feeling throughout I have blundered and erred, and the lamp of intuition I held was often dim or went out altogether. I delayed too long, and things I would have spoken about have died away in remote distances of soul.

In my retrospective meditation I could recall form or circumstance, but could not arouse vivid feeling about them once more in myself. But I think the problems arising over imagination and poetry ought to be discussed, not merely by those psychologists who have themselves neither imagination nor poetry, and are without experience, but by those who have a higher imagination than mine and a keener analytic faculty, so that the element of magic and wonder about even the lightest motions of mind might be made manifest.

Even if we do not come to unity with the spirit, there is a great gain from this meditation in which we try by a divine alchemy to transmute the gross into the subtle and pure, for very soon our whole being begins to circle around an invisible sun, and we are drawn more and more to it; and though it may be aeons before we come nigh it, yet we feel as Adam might have felt—the outcast from Paradise—after long penitence, if he had seen faintly flickering through the outer darkness of the world in which he labored the shining of the lost Eden, and knew it was not altogether lost but was accessible after purification. To have this surety is no light thing. Though we fall and fail times without number, there are hours of resurrection when the fallen angels of the heart begin to wear again their ancient angel faces, and we are melted in an anguish of exquisite joy, knowing that the dead may rise. Or earth itself may become living and play with us, and we may know what lovely allies there are for us in wood, rock, mountain, hollow of air, or along the silent shores.

Now the quietude of earth
Nestles deep my heart within,
Friendships new and strange have birth
Since I left the city's din.

Here the tempest stays its guile,
Like a big kind brother plays,
Romps and pauses here awhile
From its immemorial ways.

Now the silver light of dawn,
Slipping through the leaves that fleck
My one window, hurries on,
Throws its arms around my neck.

Darkness to my doorway hies,
Lays her chin upon the roof,
And her burning seraph eyes
Now no longer keep aloof.

And the ancient mystery
Holds its hands out day by day,
Takes a chair and croons with me
By my cabin built of clay.

OTHER TITLES OF RELATED INTEREST
FROM LARSON PUBLICATIONS

The Notebooks of Paul Brunton

Vol. 1 Perspectives

Vol. 2 The Quest

Vol. 3 Practices for the Quest/Relax and Retreat

Vol. 4 Meditation/The Body (sold as two volumes in softcover)

Vol. 5 Emotions and Ethics/The Intellect

Vol. 6 The Ego/From Birth to Rebirth

Vol. 7 Healing of the Self/The Negatives

Vol. 8 Reflections on My Life and Writings

Vol. 9 Human Experience/The Arts in Culture

Vol. 10 The Orient

Vol. 11 The Sensitives

Vol. 12 The Religious Urge/Reverential Life

Vol. 13 Relativity, Philosophy, and Mind

Vol. 14 Inspiration and the Overself

Vol. 15 Advanced Contemplation/The Peace Within You

Vol. 16 Enlightened Mind, Divine Mind

The Multiple States of Being René Guénon

An Open Life Joseph Campbell & Michael Toms

Paul Brunton: A Personal View Kenneth Thurston Hurst

Looking Into Mind Anthony Damiani

At the Leading Edge Michael Toms

For additional information, to order, or to receive a free catalog, please write Larson Publications, 4936 Route 414, Burdett, New York 14818, or call at (607) 546-9342 between 8 a.m. and 5 p.m. Eastern Time.